Pieces to a Dream

Pieces to a Dream

Kevin Wright

iUniverse, Inc.
New York Bloomington Shanghai

Pieces to a Dream

iUniverse books may be ordered through booksellers or by contacting:

iUniverse
1663 Liberty Drive
Bloomington, IN 47403
www.iuniverse.com
1-800-Authors (1-800-288-4677)

Because of the dynamic nature of the Internet, any Web addresses or links contained in this book may have changed since publication and may no longer be valid.

ISBN: 978-0-595-51979-8 (pbk)

ISBN: 978-0-595-62096-8 (ebk)

Printed in the United States of America

Acknowledgements

I'm back with my second go around. First up was "Far from Home" that introduced me to the world. This book is something special, near and dear to my heart. A man before I was a boy, walked before I could crawl, and as weird as it seems this is how my life has progressed from my walk in life. My voice is something more of a significance because I have been published so now my worth has grown. Truth be told I just want to grow through this world itself whether it be politics, schools, kids, animals, the birds and the bees. They all have something to give, they give to life just as much as any living creature alive today. There are many tears in my words, and my voice sings deeper than it speaks.

Some people are under the impression of me disconnecting from the very city I grew up in? Not the case I love my city, always have and always will. They say I have a lot of wars brewing up and I have lost touch with my home base. Its been addressed so please read on and choose your own path. Lost love was found yet not conquered but life does go on.

"Void of Course" by Jim Carroll remains near and dear to my heart as close as you will always be no matter what the circumstances. I mean no harm but the love that once was, is a has been, and given it's proper burial, put to rest on good terms. The love for the streets I will always hold deep in me as I continue to reflect on the past and the many ventures that took place just yesterday. God bless the dead hopefully we can all learn from what they died for and move on from it.

I would like to thank Trish Knudsen for her long nights in putting this project together. Krystina and Chris I could not have done this with out you in that I thank you. Amanda Costa I truly love you to pieces thank you for your support, words of encouragement, and thank you for just being a true friend. Marco and Hayden 3 Kings we did it man, stamped and approved. Tonya Kent we did it sister I love you. Kaino I love you so much I can barely come to words what you mean to me. God bless my nephews thank God your alive, please don't ever leave my side homie I need you more than you will ever know. Zee I just want to thank you for being a great friend God bless you and your family. Mary-Anne, Alisha, Anita, Sonia, Jennifer, Catherine, Charles, Pritha, Laura, Adam, Theresa, Jessica, Tanya Rego, Leandra, Shy Brat, Chris, Kerima, Lamb Laws, Julia Carter, Shakyra, Mya, Latoia, T.D., Amanda Power, Anne, my family, Chantelle, Karla, Paul, Krystal, Tamar, Lava, Lauren, Lily, Bisi, Taschena, Lovely, Calvin, Naida, Sabra, Sean, thank you all for support. Solee I love you please stay in good spirit because the sun walks in your direction gorgeous, never change and keep doing you. Sasha I love you and God bless my God daughter.

I tripped, stumbled, and I woke up from many dreams. I'm starting to understand life through my words and the many people I converse with on a day-to-day basis. I am hoping to become a jewel in that jewelry box, a figment of your imagination, twinkle in your eye, most importantly something to look forward to in life. The story itself is not over I hope to continue to create a hunger with in each and every person to want more in life. My single most important goal with this book was to create a distinctive voice and that I have done. Thank you all love live life.

I've lived life
I've suffered
I've been through fire
I've been back

Many things I've surpassed
Many yet to grasp
Many things seen
Many I have not
I've bled
I've felt pain
I've cried
I've been down

I am but beneath you
Nothing more
I lay there
Bottomless pit
Hovered over me

Nothing but dirt
Your vision
Nothing but despise
Your feeling

Never fear
For I lay
Dead beneath you
For you to crowd
Your head such evil thoughts

My heart, which is broken
My soul, which you have taken
You have taken half of me
Which you cannot see
My love for you is deep
That you did sweep
Your love I cherished
Which has perished
Your love I adore
That you ignore
Our life together
Is just a feather
That blew away
And didn't stay
It took its place
In holy grace
Never to return
Now adjourned

Life
The only life I know
No regret
No fear
Persevere or fail

Inner reflection
Outer reflection
My heart
My soul
This life is mine

Feel my pain
See my struggle
This is my life
So you see

Feel my footsteps
Feel my heart beat
Can you hear my heart beat?
Can you hear my footsteps?
Can you be me?

I watched a city disappear
New breed
Flesh and blood died behind the masks
Masks of different creeds
Animals started to show
Grass never got cut
Snakes showed their colors
Nature resolved many issues
Kings and queens became oppressed
Streets died
Loyalty died
Crews divided and conquered
Hands fell
Any means defeated purposes
A city disappeared
Long beyond my reach

Can you look into my eyes?
Like open doors
Can you open the locket to my heart?
Like turning the knob

Can you wake me up inside?
Awaken by your love
Can you kiss me?
Can you hold me?

Can you make it through my core?
Awaken my inner spirit
Can you save it?
As if it were dead?

Can you breath love within me?
Can you touch me inside?
Can you see within me?
Can you save me?
Above all else
Can you love me?

Walk with me
Take some time and walk with me
Take a tour with me
Take a walk into my past
Take a look at the present

Many feel the presence
Feel the fear
Feel my heart beat
The tears sweat inside
I hide so much

Walk with me
Take some time and walk with me
Take a tour with me
Take a walk into my past
Take a look at the present

Can you see what I see?
Feel everything I feel in this world?
Is everyone a snake?
Or is there some motive to everything?
Is everything for purpose?

Walk with me
Take some time and walk with me
Take a tour with me
Take a walk into my past
Take a look at the present

Take a walk into this voyage of mine
Realize why I think everyone isn't so kind
Realize why people are so hateful
So ungrateful
What's in everyone's best interest?

Is what I manifest?
I live for

Walk with me
Take some time and walk with me
Take a tour with me
Take a walk into my past
Take a look at the present

What is this so called life?
What is loyalty?
I don't recall ever noting the definition
I don't know what's real anymore

Walk with me
Take some time and walk with me
Take a tour with me
Take a tour with me
Take a walk into my past
Take a look at the present
Was that so hard?

Gift I have not
Heart I have so much
I write from this mind
This poetic mind
This poetic mind
Beautiful mind
Full of misconception
Non-beliefs
Judgmental in many ways
Just as your bodies will decay
My mind not so

Love is so precious
So beautiful
So hard to find
So divine
Quench my thirst
Fill my hunger
Be my last breath
My loss for words
Fill my heart
Be my deep soul

Come within
Feel the pain
I ask one thing
Be a part of me

Come back?
I never left
You did
My heart's been there
Been back

My heart you held once before
So preciously tight
So gentle
So secure
Forever?

Not the case
So I thought
Come back?
I never left
You did
My heart so did
Long ago

To the thugs
Hold your head
Stay strong
Life can last but a second

Guns, whips, and chains
Is no life
Dying for your hood
Nothing nice

Slugs determine realness
Real then separated from the fake
A genuine thug
Strapped without forgiveness
No heart
Breaths so much pain
Inflicted upon others

No love
Bitterness built within
Driven by that dollar
Not an inch of power
No control
With need someone to hold

The world breathes
Such jealousy and envy
Doors closed
Trust never such a thing existed
The world
A thug's world

I have so much to say
Open your ears
Listen attentively
I beg of you
But a second of your time

Read along
Figure the message
Hidden between the lines
This no rhyme

Read it
See it
Believe it
Right before your very eyes

I was such a little soul
Seeking the guidance and support
Never ended up before that very court
Stuck in the system
That life I chose never lead

I've never coped a plea
Nor expected any bargain of any sort
Never released any slugs
Never carved

Never seen the bars
Confined to a small space
Surrounded by drug dealers and killers

I am but a little soul
Under guidance
Never ended up before that very court
Stuck in the system
That life I chose never to lead

All about the rep
Yet you took one extra step
Closer to death
Testing this so called faith
Which you think you have so much

Life yet not based upon faith
But upon how you live
Roads chosen
Paths decided to walk
Journeys beckoned upon
Stars nearing closer
Closer and closer
Yet with blood sweat and tears
Still unable

Today
Yet such a special day
Not yesterday
The day before yesterday
Today

Yesterday
Yet such a beautiful day
Not tomorrow's day
Nor the day after tomorrow's day
Yesterday

Tomorrow
Yet filled with so much love
Not today, nor yesterday
Tomorrow breaths love in the air

Today yet such a special day
Yesterday yet such a beautiful day
Tomorrow yet so much love
Today, yesterday, and tomorrow

Lord above earth
In the sky
Where blue placates
Hidden amongst the clouds
Your wrath
Thunder and lightning
Heavy storm
Thumping the earth
As if we sinned

Morning a new day
You shed light on a new day
As it arrives
Perhaps a sign of better to come
Happiness fills the air
Breaths of hope
Dreams floating
Wind blowing
Sky blue as ever

Sun slowly falls
Light begins to slowly fade
Darkness is yet to fall
The moon is eminent
As it spreads its love
Bright night
Bright day
Now we must pray

I never had a father
Left a fatherless child
A bastard so to say
A mother alone
Nonetheless another statistic

Slained not my heritage
Nevertheless my heart
My soul
Undying pain
Yet an urge to love
A father figure

Nonetheless a man I am
Man I've become
Inside me
I built in me
A beating heart
Repeated pounds
Love and survival
Honor and respect
To thy mother
To thy father

My love knows no limit
Beauty of it
How it feels
Infatuated by the light
It's warmth
Burning desire
For its very existence

All alone
No one to confide in
When I sleep
When I wake

People pass through me, up, and around me
Over topple me
I am but a ghost
Ghost of bright light
Ghost of dark night

Who am I?
Can you see me?
Do I bleed?
Do I feel pain?
Can I just maybe
Just maybe, if possible die?
Am I like the rest?
What is it you presume?

Lost and so confused
To many
So many thoughts running through this thick skull of mine
So difficult to define
Too hard to decipher

Many thoughts contemplated
So many decisions to decide
So little time
I am but at mercy
A bottomless pit
Dirt filled to the chin
Smell and filled with such dirt inside to out
Left without a route

So near and dear to my pressure heart
I'm looking to find my one true love
I'm waiting for you
I spend everyday wishing for you
To walk into my life

Will I ever fully be complete?
For the love I have to share
So much care
It means so much to find you
Endure all the heartache and pain of love

I've been all around
Waiting for you
Wishing for you
Looking for you
Searched here and there
So little time to spare
I want it all
You

So many fans
The powerful media
So much of an affect on the world
If everyone knew the truth

What is home?
So many blocks corrupted
Filled with such evil
Single mothers
Kids running into the streets
Kids running for their streets
So much envy built towards supporting the blocks and projects

So much of the dollars to support the guns
So little to the schools
This thing we call culture
Whatever it is and composed
Society and media destroy the people as a whole
People the main objective
Or thought to be
Where's the justice?
Where's the love?
Filled with such warfare

People have no rest
Forever weary they are
Wondering to hear the next siren
Blue and red lights surround

On the streets they pray for better days
When the block would be worry free
Needles flooding the floors
Getting chased by the lights
Ridding of all the fights

Sleeping to such cold and dark nights
I pray and wish for better days

Can I clear the tears?
Turn off the leaky faucet
Countries drown in their own misery
The powers to be
Can I create a site to see?
Words and wisdom
Words are wisdom
If I die shall my kingdom come?
Death seems changing
Life is revolutionary
Church seems the salvation
Am I a slave harassed in my own ways?
Stimulating change seems inevitable
Peace seems severe
What makes sense?
Sense of emotion

Clear the tears

To my people
For my people
We are not oppressed
Yet filled with so much opportunity
So much to seek
To much to find
Indeed we have the guidance

We have heart and soul
Willpower so strong
To withstand any obstacle
We fall
Leap right back
Face to face

To my people
For my people
We are but equal
Separated by color, race, and collar
But we exist
With that we can't resist

Only the sky can be that limit
To reach and capture that entity
To fill that emptiness missing
It is hidden amongst the clouds
Difficult to find
But possible to reach

To my people
For my people
For we are but oppressed
With that find that nest
Hidden amongst the clouds

Can you feel my pain?
It burns so deep
The fire within
This burning blaze
Hurts so much
You have not the slightest clue

Feed not off my fire
It burns with a destructible desire
Smoke contaminating your lungs
Choking, coughing
A wish for a fresh breathe of air
If you only knew how it could tear
Tears me apart within
I can't give in

I have so much fight
In the deepest of nights
Though so bright
This fire burns such a blaze
So much courage, faith, love
Deep within my cores
I have not the slightest bit of death in me
If you could only see

I been down without you
I can't sleep at night
Holding my pillow so late
Never so laid back
My mind has such an attack
Filled with such empty thoughts
Mindless in such ways
No pictures
Vivid thoughts jump at me
Blinded I see nothing

I don't want to be alone
Alone without you
Full of such content
My heart will not plummet
For I am filled with such care within
This deep love
I share for you
One day you will see
As if bright light
Has shunned your deep blue eyes

I can do it
If you want it
I can do it
Your dreams and deepest fantasy
I can reach your deepest core
Touch you
Stroke you over and over
Over again

Put you in the mood
Don't get too confused
Believe me I can be very crude
Your clothes just lose them
Take them off fast or slow
Strip if necessary
I can be unnecessary

I can reach your utmost peak
Just let me seek
Touch your heart
Cause you to yearn for more
No questions it's your way
I'm here to stay

Seek your spot
Believe me it'll get hot
From your neck
Down your spine
Oh you're so mine
I can be kind
So gentle
Rough and tough
Baby so hard

It's easy to look at my life
An see no pain
Switching from lane to lane
You could never understand this pain
It drives me so insane
This pain hurts so deep
My core cannot withstand
At times I thought I was the man

It's easy to look at my life
An see no frustration
So many breathes of frustration
Driving me so crazy inside
Feelings of such hatred within
Waiting to burst onto the world
Most times I sit and curl

It's easy to look at my life
An see no mind
For which you have the trouble to define
You have no idea
At times I feel as though it isn't even mine
Most times I see between the lines
People so unkind

It's easy to look at my life
An see no pain
Sense the frustration that builds within
Yet see no mind so out of control
Someday I may unfold

Sick and tired of the one night stands
Disgusted in you, you, and you wanting me to be your man
Stop fooling with my mind
Your love you can't define
My love you cannot obtain
This isn't a gift from god
I've come too far to have my heart broken
My love cannot be bought
Just a thought
There is a way
Pitch the realness
Hide not in closed closets
Behind closed doors
Keep it real
You be you
I be me
Then you may see

The essence of beauty
I cannot describe
It remains a thought on my mind
But if I must try
To explain a piece of the pie

Kind sweet gestures
A warm hug
A kiss to touch your spine
An make your soul quiver
A presence felt in the room
The smell of sweet perfume

The sweet in your tea
Causing you to plea
The twisting knot in your stomach
Causing your heart to plummet
Beat at vast speeds
She is one of your biggest needs

The essence of beauty
I cannot describe
It remains a thought on my mind

Cry me a river
Full of tears
Flooding the streets
Pouring through the cracks
Filling the sewers cracking the pipes
Smashing car windows

Feel my pain
Witness my misery
You can never see
How much my heart pleas

Inside my mind
So hard to define
I try to find a place of rest
This continues to remain a test
So many thoughts unexplained
Awake I am
Awake I feel not
Trapped in a maze
Which sometimes I feel is a phase

I suffered many years
Shed so many tears
Cry me a river
Watch me shiver
I'm lost in weary
Forever query
Light me a match
Lead the way
For I've been lead astray

My destiny is living well
But Feel within hell

My every step is calculated
For I feel as though I haven't made it

Shed so many tears
For times the end seems near
Living this life of pain
Feeling of nothing to gain
Visions of leaving this world in a Hurst
My life seems cursed

Such a struggle to survive
If only I had some guide
I don't want to see the chalk lines
For I have been given that sign
I don't want to suffer no more

My life full of so many bad decisions
So indecisive so unpredictable
Sometimes inexplicable
What's it like?
To be in love

Something I can't buy
Many moments feel like the wrong time
But I want to climb
That love mountain
Though I cannot find it
Where does this life go for me?
I can't even fathom to see
I'm slowly finding out
What it's all about
I feel like I'm going mad
Feelings for one I once had
My heart is open to seek and find
Waiting for something to come to mind
Something to be mine
Just one a kind is all I hope
I wish I could see through the microscope

Open my mind
Open my heart
Cease my soul
It's ready to unfold
I feel left out in the cold

Take me in
Let it all begin
I feel like this is a sin
Please get under my skin
I'm ready to win

Lose it all
Let it all fall
Your cloths to the floor
What's the score?
Your shirt your pants
Let me get a glance
What a sight to see
This body to be
Mine yours so what's the score?
I want more

So beautiful
So divine
Let me creep your spine
This love isn't one of kind
Just one to be mine
Unlike like no other
Yours to discover
Not a chance
You get but a glance
Beauty is sensuous
So voluptuous

A kiss to touch your heart
Cleanse your soul

Open my mind
Open my heart
Cease my soul
It's ready to unfold
I feel left out in the cold

You bleed just like me
Cry just like me
You see not what I see
Nor be what I want to be

The sky not my limit
Nor is there a mountain that I want to climb
Nor is there a ladder of success
Though I do get depressed

This is real life
My life right in front of me
I can't fathom to see the future
Though I do hope bright
I have no sight but vision
Dream so to say
With that I must pay
My dues hard times and tribulations
In order to succeed

So repeat
Repeat I must
To gain that trust
Trust in my heart and soul
To reach my goal
I care not about the sky
Nor these high mountains
You see not what I see
Nor where I want to be

Remember back in the days
Take a trip down memory lane
Life so was so insane
The many times we tried to pull weight
Barely enough to feed ourselves
We were two soldiers
Two soldiers at one with ourselves
We were all about us

Remember all the cowards
So fake to them
Always wanting to spar
They swear they were stars

The time we ran from the cops
Through the fields jumping the fences
We swore it was the trenches
Not to mention
All the girls drooling
We were inseparable
Troopers
Just trying to live

I'm not a mime
I don't read between the lines
Can't u understand this life of mine
Almost caught a brain tumor
Trying to escape the rumors
I am but one soul
So many intentions
Not to mention
Stop making me the center of attention

I am what you will never understand
Never be understood
Yet generalized or categorized
Please don't apologize
Better yet wish for my demise
I am everything but an angel

All the denies
So many apologies
None accepted
So many disrespected
No point intended

So many names claimed
You swore to key to my fame
I hit the zone
Week in week out
You no where about
I'm a soldier a trooper
I never thought I knew you
Make no mistake this isn't for you
I introduced myself to this world

I'm at odds trying to escape my grave
The sight to which I lay dead
So many dreams
So many nightmares
I don't know how my life will be
How will it end?

Let me write
I want to write
If I may repent
Let me repent
Let me speak
I want to speak
Let my voice be heard
I want to be heard
Let my actions be seen
Let me be seen
Let me cry
Do not dry my tears
Let me bleed
I don't want to bleed
Le t me die
For I was born to

I have so much heart
A heart that burns for that abundance of success
Yet the streets have me oppressed
The authority figures think they know everything
Yet they know not a thing
So much knowledge
So brilliant minded yet no heart
They see within their eyes
Discouraging my thoughts
Crushing my dreams
No provision of hope
Lacking that guidance and support
Providing no experience

I've seen it in my eyes
Been through the hell and storm
That became my norm
I've been through the pain and suffering
You have no idea
Fathom to even think my life
You would not have such a clue

My life always at odds
Never defying God
So confused all these years
Through the many tears
I grew up from being a boy
To what I am now a man
Never receiving it well
Never choosing this life
But this life chose me

The rumors have been obsessed with me
No matter where I went
The time spent
I've been through it all
I've had my share of falls
Ups and downs
My life been turned around
Taken its twist and turns
Flips so many I can't recall
My life has come to a straight stall
So many denials
So many regrets
So many hard pills to swallow
My life was once shallow

Mind, reality, and dreams
So hard to separate
The difference between them
The unsettled differences
The story behind everything
So called untold tale about two who were in love
Never ending within each others heart
Destined to cross paths once again
The time has come within the dreams
The constant reminders come to mind
Reality needs to be written
For it once was
An someday again forever

Make no mistake about it
Any block can be laid to rest
For that matter put to sleep
It can rain
It can pour rain
Blood leaves a stain
Thicker than water
A bullet can change a life
Face imprinted on tomorrows paper
Making the headlines

My best friend
My companion
I've never been hit
Never been broke
Attached is that lens, that scope
Special view to your heart
Detecting fear and hurt
Bottling up all that blood within
Seizing every single breath in you

We've been here before
Never been hit
Info red dot point blank
He has no heart
The devil corrupts his pity soul
Blood flows the vein
Like no one else
He breathes not a single breath of air
He smokes leaving traces
Destination elsewhere
Hell or heaven

He plays his position
Sometimes the best of company
That secret stash
He feels the heat
Before it arrives
His slender body
Shine as chrome
Never wanting to leave home

I feel like I'm growing extinct
The best alive seems far fetched
I remain content in my ways
Failing to realize the important things in life
The love of it all is missing
The abundance for more
The past seems forever haunting my every step
The future seems blooms
My heart is bruised but I'll live
Dad is about to die
My heart follows along with him
The pain of it all
A fatherless child
Kid who walked before he crawled
If i die
Let off the shots
I need no introduction
I've done more than a block itself
Music to my ears
My words are placed above it all
Cheers to life
I love you
Goodbye

Growing Extinct

You see within my inner circle
Blood, sweat, and tears
So many years fought constant reminders
So many pictures painted upon my walls
Stained colors traceable
Leading back to once was
Seeing the past
Not letting a single day pass by
Look at life
Not through with it

Pictures have not passed
Nor has all the memorable memories
Nothing seems tainted
Love wanting forever more
The understanding so deep and precious
Voice so heart warming
Telephone rings with such a heartbeat
Life on the other side of things
Once one had
Love speaks this name

Take a walk with me
In my dream everything seems so perfect
Wonderful and kind love seems
No fear no regret seem evident
Above water we are
No gasping for air
Alive we are more than ever before

Take a look at my life
Filled with your every presence
The essence of your beauty
The unremarkable scent of you
And your sunshine you deliver when never could be done

Take a look at me
I'm so frustrated
Hurting within me
I need that light once again
Take me your way once again
Your love seems destined again
Our souls seem destined again

Heard your voice
I wish could
You fulfill my ever-burning desire
My every complete dress attire
My soul feels on fire
Such the spark of your voice
Ignites a flame within
Stem so deep but able to make contact
Ablaze creating heat
I crawl to knees in defeat

Visions of once being there
Cloud nine where you were mine
Child in love
Something I discovered in someone so beautiful
Love once knew me
Keeping my world intact
My heart a complete match
My heart open filled with so much abundance
Burning deep for your every existence
Everything about you
What made you, you
What made us a perfect match?
What made us detach
Two hearts not spoken
Left so much to say
Words so meaningful

Girl next door
Just a walk away
Love in my life
Love of my life
Love so spiritually deep
Heart so pure
A soul to cherish

Girl next door
Not a bridge too far to cross
So true to life
So many views to life
Such a mind to life
Such so many thoughts
Such an action

Girl next door
Closer than a phone call away
To my dismay
So full of life
So full of love
Love is life
Love is my every existence

I'm neither dead nor gone
I am the witness of my every shadow
My every movement is a calculated step
I bear witness to my past
Not knowing what lies in store
What awaits me?
Yet to be determined

I know not my complete sense of self
But my every thought and things
My corruption, frustration, what affects me
I know not my full mind capacity
But an idea of mind process

I stand witness to my every dream
For I was there
In my world where it took place
In the caves, fields, red, yellow, and black roses
Witnessing death
I died but reality awakes my soul from dreams
I stand before you neither dead nor gone

I am everything but different
I am what I am
What you see
The object as it appears before your very eyes
A nigger black, bold, and beautiful
So much to say so it does not appear
Take some time out
Listen

One life to live
Letting not a day pass by
So many days dark and confused
Mentally and spiritually dead at times
More days have transgressed this rhyme

This is the life
High as ever no hydro
So much to never ignore
Intoxicated by the struggle
So many trying times
As days go by they progress this rhyme

One life to live
This is the life
So much to claim
Living up to the name
As that pulse beats by

You cannot fathom to figure it out
The just of it
A piece of the pie
An inkling of it
Why it happens?
What takes place visually?

That soul emerging to the sky
Why it is the way it is
Why life can glitter at a particular moment
The next just seem like forever rain
Filled with dying pain
Plenty of suffocation
A yearn for oxygen
The gist of a single breathe
To survive that need

Death comes
Splurging that explosion of importance
Too late the coffin has arrived
Too little too late
That undying love has awoken
Eating within the depths of your core
Ever so alive
That it is, life as it is known

The talk of the streets
Leaving many to weep
In their pity and shame
I relish off this abundance of success
They think I am repressed even oppressed
Say what you say
Claiming whatever it is you dare
I've shed so many tears
So wide-open, a public
This is but a public appeal
I am everything but steel

I've born witness to those dark nights
Cold days
I've been through the storm
Never dearly departed
They say home is where the heart is
I am everywhere but home
In hopes one day I will be there
One day

I am what the streets claim me to be
Everything and anything they could possibly claim
I've persevered I've failed on front the eye
My heart has died
I've been shocked back to life
I've been down on bended knee
I've been in the case of particular pleas

I feel that undying pain
Never showing that fear
For I fear not death itself
For death will come upon me
Till my dying day
Ceasing never to exist
I will stand tall

10 toes as well 10 fingers
I am human no alien
Just different in so many ways
So many to describe
Despite my capability it has not been seen
They've looked within my eyes
Shedding was their perspective of me
Everything they could possibly see
Nothing ever displayed
Though it did
Blinded it was
For I was everything that they saw
Everything they made me to be

I am claiming no set
Earning my respect the old fashion way
A fusion of just being me
Not my choice of self
Claiming no line or face
Living me and nothing though me

Being me from the days of cradle
Till my days of unburied grave
Looking to the sky
For it holds everything that it prosperous for me
In me
My dreams fly for me ride
Amongst the clouds
For there is my purpose
Claiming me and no set
A fusion for just being me

There is so much injustice
Failing to define this justice of injustice
For justice has not been served with any explanation
Explaining justice has not been reiterated
Taken into consideration for that matter
For there is so much injustice
Not enough justice to explain the injustice

The ghetto seems to have a mental telepathy that no one seems they can escape For they have been blinded by that particular image of life that they see for it all everything within this life is them. For they know not nothing but this and or what they have been exposed to. So much imagery, dreams, and the nightmares that have them secluded eating their life as we see away. They walk with everything but purpose and particular goal, surviving each and everyday seems to be their means of living. Feeding that empty stomach, feeding off whatever knowledge that blows within the wind that happens to surpass them by. Lost souls seem to fly but not the dreams for that odd reason, maybe oppression for that system seems to be putting bars before them limiting success providing that sense of boundary. In that brings on the years of coming depression for people are not equal but different and that's what separates them. They see not what they see but what others envision and that follows painting pictures of what they see forbidding looking within own self to find that meaning to life.

Stand still listen to this game we play of hard knocks, shots beat this block
Hitting a few who live by that lead taking that step forward they die by lead.
Continuing that forcing hand risking losing their closest man. The circle refuses
to live by the almighty bible, this life is all that is known. Behind bars laying with
a confession on their head plate refusing to snitch but to let their brother enjoy
his freedom while they await destiny that lies in the hands of the lord. It seems
that circle has a mental telepathy, new breed regains the position of old breed
continuing with no sense of change. Corrupted by what they see and not by the
many dreams that float, committing life to nothing as it seems but is everything
to them, what sense is there to visualize?

Contemplated decisions
Confused thoughts
Love in the air
Such a fear
Such a scare
My love is so sincere

I see deep within you
Deep within your care
A love for me so precious
So divine
Pure, deep, sweet

I've awaken within you
Awaken that sensitive side
Untouched love
Your care for me so steep
Your heart racing
Pounding, drumming, plummeting
So weak

My kiss, my touch
So true it is
My words false
Not true
These words I spew
Straight to your soul
To touch, hold, keep
I have everything it is you seek

Money, power, respect
Destination heaven
The power of the dollar
Holds so much cruelty and wickedness
Blood, sweat, and tears
Leak away as it passed through
Death and poverty
Hunger and malnutrition
Dreadful frustration
Leaving so many words to mumble
But to whom?
Is that it?
So called development
So it is or perceived to be
So we shall
Or have we?
The time seems to have past?
Bark with on any doorstep
Development they say
The roles they portray
People mislead
Development promoted but not fed
The people must die
The people must die
So they say

I've been withholding my anger
Refraining from committing to that stranger
That someone who seems to exist deep within
He pushes and he pulls for existence
Hounding boisterously
No backing down without a fight

Representing the flip side of things
Playing the opposite wing
On his guard ready to strike at will
To kill if necessary
Standing for everything that is not
Nothing that is meant to be

As time passed
Nearing closer and closer to his demise
He remains closer in disguise
The flame slowly dies
Perishing ever so slowly
Till it is a flame no more

I'm living my dream, who ever thought I be in this position to share this with so many souls. I'm out here with a muscle but my hands not tied behind my back. They may have my tongue-tied but they cannot stop me from writing this peace of mind and this freedom of mine. So on that let me speak this moment of clarity, share with you all. I'm building this mind, muscle, through this struggle that I aim to concur with out any missile to lead me to this zone. Relying upon myself and myself alone. Others have failed in proving they can coexist with me along my journey to stardom by committing to so many actions. The actions they proclaim I want no part of that is why I want no one to take a walk with me. I journey to the unknown to such a land, dream, and memory whatever it is I aim to find it. I know not what I'm looking for when I find it I will know.

I am, I am
I am whatever it is I am
I am whatever it is I want to be
I am whatever it is you see
I am your wildest imagination
I am your selfless dream
I am whatever it is you see deep within your core
I am everything and a score for sure

Angel believes that she envisions what appear before her very eyes me. She envisions I live this life above water fighting for every breath of oxygen that I can bear to stomach from my lungs. I am in this fight amongst myself where this battle between mind and self seem to collide in altercation. I was a man before I became a child forced to pick up his soother, run before walk, speak before spoken to, learn with no resource. Spell before I learn to read, teaching myself everything I could possibly imagine. I patted myself on the back when no one was there when I stretched needing that sense of comfort and understanding most important support. Angel forsee's so much in me in a result to her generalization of me toward me.

They can't stop me from writing can they? I got too much on my heart right now. I apologize if anything becomes unclear from this point in; I'm steering in the mirror as I write this with an image of not me but my mind, body, and soul. This seems like history in the making for me. I cannot speak but my fingers are mobile so let the jungle city kid speak because when I die that's what I was and still am and forever will be. The kids run in the streets with there pampers strapped at their side mother chasing in hand a belt to fix that tail. It seemed like growing up in jungle city it had a mental telepathy. Some of the young bloods became dead bloods and it continued. The young gifted became nothing but a street statistic whom had that promising future ahead of themselves but for one split second were able to trade it in for a gun an a badge to represent our city strip. However I choose to represent it in a different manner. So many poetic verses I choose to spit of my memories, life in the fast lane, life in the dark, many wishes in which I had, the misery that I saw, all the abuse and so much more letting my strip know that I got this. It was labeled jungle city back in the early 80's, my home, home is where the heart is, home is where my heart is.

I did not start this shit
But I will finish it if dared
I strike fear within your eyes
Believe me I can pop a surprise
I'm a blessing in disguise
It so simple to take your life
You have not a clue
Want to be gangster
Wake up and make up
You done fucked up now

So innocent such a soul
Fighting within herself
Mind and heart trying to console
That you help unfold
Fuck this relationship we threw
You have no idea who I am
Business can become war
War leads to death
To your demise I can foresee
Everyone around you better fear me
The devil within me feels full control
All I need to do is point
You can get smoked like grown weed

What bothers me the most you still continue
I wish death upon no man
My blood sweat and tears is building
This anger and frustration I keep concealed within
It's boiling to begin
As we grow as men
We learn to let a lot go
But there is so much bullshit that I withstand
You can only step upon my toes so few times

I have no rep to withhold
Now I'm talking to you straight
Lets not let this situation escalate
Or a so-called soldier will be buried
The ground humbling your acceptance
I would love to see your resignation
Placed upon your life
A penny lies above your head
Your worth a bucket shit
I'm prepared to die for this
Ask yourself the same question
I got nothing to lose
Your death to gain

One night involved such intimacy
Oil dripping downs your sweet skin
Through the crease of your spine
Flowing ever so smoothly
Down you're your back as it hits my palm

Stroking my hand up and down
Side to side
Across, back down, and up again
Nibbling upon your ear
Whispering such soft sweet words
Causing knots within
Conceiving you to give in
To my warmth and comfort
My lips ever so soft
Your lips brushing across
Breathing such energy of sympathy
Such a symphony
Such music flows
Soft brush kisses
Painted upon you lips

I want to see you smile
I want to be the reason you smile
I want you not in denial
You are my princess
Every inch of my core
My heart and soul forever more

I want to see you smile
I want to be the reason you smile
I want to be every phone calls you dial
You are my ever thought
My every dream
Star I look at as dark beckons upon me
You're all that I see
You're the reason I smile
I want to be the reason you smile

I've been critically claimed everything that could be
Everything that the world foresees
I am everything that has been perpetuated
    Undressed in the public eye
To some a blessing in disguise
Made a mockery deemed a coward
In that the public breaths such sour thoughts
In the past I've become a lost thought
I've fought and growled and scratched my way to the surface
Going back I've forbidden doing

I've been stained
My name spit upon
In that I've begun
To show signs of life and recovery
Fighting to live
Even though I'm living to die
Fighting to see
Though I see nothing inside
Fighting to give
But not blessed with the opportunity
I'm living to find
Whatever and whomever it is
In that I seek
I seek and I shall find

Pass me a pen
Get me a pad
Let me speak through this pen
Let me spit through this pen
If I can and if I may
Can I tell you the stories displaced?
If I can
Can I vent for a minute
In my moment of clarity
In that I expose all my sincerity
Sincerely to those who take a offence to the words written
To them I do not spit upon
But reveal my side
Hearing both sides
The object in the mirror is my reflection
Failing to see me holding within its grasp the physical form
Connecting with me not spiritually and mentally
Physically it can see me
But within me
It is and never will be me
It cannot envision me
But me
Make sense it doesn't
It fails to see the object of affection
The object attention
It holds me within the physical form

They paint the many pictures
The little fish in a big pond
They depict me to be
Figuring I'm through with it
I got the mind of a hustler
Heart of king
I've seen myself to the endless struggle
Hoping for brighter days
Failing to pay me my respect garnered
I continue to walk the streets
Searching for the unknown
Fighting to live
Dying to give
Misery seems to be my state of mind
I'm remain destined to find
A peace of mind
This heart of mine
Through hell, fire, and brimstone
Gladly risking it all

I gladly risk it all
Life or death the case
As it may be
My life on the line
In these trying times of pain and suffocation
No time to breath
In this struggle to succeed
Not making a dime
Walking that thin red line
Through love and hate
Jealously and envy that so many embody
Looking at what I embody
The truth in me
The truth is I
There's no escape
I must see it

Live from the red stop signs and yellow lines
Where graffiti placates my mind
So many seem to find that state of mind
The struggle between conscious and decision
The fight in reality and dream
Depicting the difference among them

Where smoke crowds the air
Getting paid was the way raised
Living by any means necessary
Popping shot pellets relentless
Many times left penny less
Putting tracks to life
Displacing life off track

The hard struggle growing up in housing
Many walking heads low
No faith
Authority believing life was at odds
So many critically acclaimed frauds
I am a street calculus
I know my math
Cheating my way through life
So they perceived
So it is to be
I the streets
Like yellow lines on concrete
Stand before you
Making sense out of emotion

This is dedicated to the streets
The streets I am
The streets is within me
The streets raised me
Now I'm immune to it
It's all I got

I've walked the dog
I've been clouded in the found
The deep mist has crowded me
The streets have corrupted my mind
The media has painted a dark image
Poverty has lead me to believe
Africa finds it hard to survive
Sudan is concerned with funds
Building an economy is no solution
The people have no word
When they die so goes hope
Life is left afloat
Swimming for survival
No concerns no worries
People left in a weary
This life seems so scary
I have no one near me
So many fail to see
I stand flooded in tears
Wondering when things are going to change
Hopefully in so many years

They've taken away my hunger
Left me with greed
Made me not a leader
Shedding no light on me
Forcing me to fight
Leaving me with no guided sight
To lead me, guide me
This is my life
My life alone

Made me a leader
Before I was ready to lead my own
I left many disown
Things are not always as they seem
The past seems written
I continue to write everyday
Everyday seems a new chapter
Left for the soul to capture
I talk it like I live it
This is I
All I

My life full of ink and paper that fills this very book containing my life, my very existence of who I am and what makes me. Life means alive and death seems eternal sleep. My life based on some many values and beliefs, living to my dying day, providing a sense of hope to this dying breed who seem to be lost thoughts beaten out of their own minds and appear to be what they not know. I am what you not know but what you see. When I die I hope to have sparked a few minds and create bond by my words and peace of mind. I was always destined to represent and leave a stench never to be forgotten. This is my life!

The sky will fall
The sun will die
Not a day to survive
7 days will cease to exist
Pitch black
Not a moon to hover over
No light
Our hearts and soul to disappear
While darkness inherits the earth

Always content
To uplift another soul
Rise above all
Concur my greatest fears
While following in the steps of my heart
Capturing my dreams
Wishing on a shooting star
Take advantage of par
Seize the moment

Infatuated with love
Everything about it
The many elements as many potions
As many mixes
The many procedures
As many corrections
Love
The experiment
Or so presumed to be

If I die
Don't you dare send me flowers
I rather a fire
In memory
Acknowledging my existence
Symbolizing my heart
Its brightness and passion to burn
Flames throughout the night
Till morning sunrise
Reminiscing me forever

My heart will never die
In each one of you
Lies my undying spirit
To be with you every step of the way
Till together again

I see you
What do you see?
Your mind a daze
You delusional
Multiple personalities
Which to decide next?

I see you
What do you see?
You look up
Clouded in darkness filled with emptiness
Where to go?

I see you
What do you see?
Crowding your head
Empty thoughts
Drowning in tears no apparent reason
What do you long for?

I haven't been blessed with this so-called gift. I have a deep passion to express this mind I have, let me tell you I find it quite intriguing. My life as an intellectual though not accepted in this fashion. I always appreciated what was good for my mind and didn't accept the many things I strongly disliked. A lot became of no importance to me; take it how you want to take it.

Love of my life
Lone star in the sky
Sun in my morning
My moon at night
Forever shining
Every hope
Every thought
Every wish
Every dream
My pillow at night
I hold ever so tight
A love so fine
Forever to be mine

Sometimes I forget who I am, my place in this world, and then come to the realization that this is my life because it keeps occurring. All this brings about is anger and frustration while I'm dreaming in this imaginative world I try to build in my mind. The perfect family, perfect relationship, and so on. I come to the realization that this world is imperfect and I had to accept that. Make no mistake I value and cherish everything that I have forth me its just sometimes it all feels short. I just have to learn to accept life as it comes.

My star shines bright at night
My moon sleeps so peacefully
My sun eats away at my skin
Leaving its hot remarks
Cold leaves me to quiver
Snow is as beautiful as it comes
Gently touching my soft skin
The cold I embrace
As it causes me to shiver with a steer
Knowing beauty is beautiful
Right before me
As I stare within

Black is darkness
Black I sleep to at night
Black is me
Black my eyes
Black my hair
Black my culture
Black for me
Black is me
Black is forever
Black I is I forever

The day will rise I cease to exist
Long before earth disappears
Long before god himself graces the world with his presence
Burn three candles
All of different color
All different shape size and form
Different scent
Time span three days
Morning to night
Dusk till dawn knowing that I'm gone
Envision me in your mind
That divine human being
Self righteous and respectful
Privileged and successful
Honored thy mother thy father
Bringing me into this crazed beautiful world

Now dying in peace
Heavens to uplift and unfold
Hell to bow beneath the lord
Take my soul so precious
My flesh left behind
Eaten away bits and bites
Till no more
I am free
Mind body and soul

Locked up 1 year
2 years
It seems like 5 to life
They caught you
Confiscated the shotty
Beating you senseless resisting arrest
So proclaimed

That is who you are
Never failing to express emotion
Never backing down
That was never an option in your vocabulary
That lion heart was born within
Symbolizing that courage respect honor and loyalty
To the red stop signs and yellow lines
That left many to slain
Live and die for the streets
Blood sweat and tears
Never expressing fear

The ink is running out
I can no longer scream and shout
Never again to visit
My words sealed together
Take to heart
The penitentiary is no home
It is never to life
Home sweet home awaits you
Peace and one love

So many from a far through darts my way
As if I were a target
Not mentioning my speech
This lisp that I project
So many words I have to say
So many words unheard
Not being heard was a solution not a suggestion
Can I be heard?
Can I live?
I considered a spade a spade
It is what it is
Not fake as real as it comes
As real as it is delivered
So real to life
Confused with conceited
I am what I depicted to be
Life in the flesh
The pain and agony I express
In that what a success
I feel not oppressed
I've left my nest
Breathing in this wonderful world of happiness

Ink is my Pacifier

Ink is my pacifier
As I sit and think
The past and the future
The presence has me engaged
The future I want to marry
The past I don't ever want to forget
I want to abolish slavery
Though it'll never end I remain content on seeing it through
I wish Martin still existed
I'm stuck with his inspirational words
It doesn't seem enough these days
I value the air I breathe
The people I speak to seem jaded
I sit and think about life and my expression
The lisp is foolish
The pen is incredible
The ink sways so deep
The government on the bill
I have no interest in
I just want to live and see life through
I remain prepared to die tomorrow
Whether they have a bullet for me or not
I'm ready for anything these days

I put it in ink
I remain strong more powerful than Malcolm
No dis-respect
I hear the blasts
I live in this world of wars, disputes, and words
I remain at one with myself
I falter at times with such a big heart
I become too deep
A solid figure on the outside
I cry on the inside
I miss love so much
I miss the past love
I create too much these days
To which I cannot bear
It's not always black and white these days
The world is more intertwined
The roots pierce deeper

Set of two very few could match
Caliber and prestige
Such beauty and elegance
Voluptuous lips
Smooth faces
Light skin
Appearance so gentle
Long beautiful hair
Black shine
Such display of beauty
Curls of sensation
All shriveled and bunched
Complicated in so many ways

Let me release you
Your inner soul
Who you are
What I seek
Every bit and inch
Every ounce

Afraid of love
Everything about it
Its touch
Its scent and fragrance
Its very existence
Be not afraid of me
Nor my love
Touch me
Hold me
Kiss me
Fear nothing

Let me die today
Forget that I ever existed
My life just a lost thought
Forget my very existence

I don't want the world to see me
I don't think that they would understand
Everything is made to be broken
My heart
My ties
My life
Let me die today
Forget my very existence
A lost thought
A distant memory
Let me drift away

I my own man
I make own decisions
I walk the path
Chosen lead by me
I walk the valley
So many men and women
What makes me different?

Indeed I am
So many ways leave me distinct
Ways in which indescribable
Indescribable to myself
As well to others
Others depict me to be different
Different in manner and style
Style of mind
Style of mine
Mind is mine
Mine I own
Me is me
You is you
They are they
We are we

Oppressed by the streets
Oppressed by authority
I'm oppressed by my mind
My heart and soul
Everything in me
To the bitter end
Life's a gift
A privilege so to say
You're here today
Not here tomorrow
Live from the cradle to the grave
Sun to the moon
To the stars at night
Risk yes
Fear no
Flowers bloom
People grow
In life you never know

A life is born
A life taken
Nothing seems mistaken
Everything seems reason
People seek the greed and envy
The glory and prestige
I value existence
My life so to say
My friends love me
My enemies hate me
I am I
I can only be me

See me discreet
Discover me silent and motionless
Eyes pale
Body cold as ice
Feel the shiver
Perspiration at a high
A Negro dead
Body decay
Feel my heart thump
Open my eyes
All but a flashback
A figment of your imagination
Just a memory
I'm dead now

I am but a flower growing between the depths of concrete, mysterious but strange looking branch ever so slowly. I am but a stem a leaf that blows so swiftly. I am nothing short of spectacular; I am what I am but a flower growing between the depths of concrete.

Stand forward for it I nothing special but a genuine man, a young man spreading his poetic justice, a love to write and rhyme. I write this love, expressing this creative mind, this poetic mind, similar to a love for music. I stay in tune with the belief of freedom for expression and a love for what I do.

Bless my mind
Bless my soul
My heart
Which endures all pain
My mind I express
My soul I exert
My heart I elevate
True faith I believe in
Death is a must

I seemed destined since birth
Destined to shine within my own spotlight
Even when they turned off the light
Locking me in the cage that became too deep
Leaving me frustrated and hurt inside
So many have tried
So many have died
Things are not always what they seem to be
In the darkness light has dawned upon me
Leading me not through the bars
But mind at ease and at rest
Resulting in salvation
They've controlled me physically
In attempts to leave me mentally impaired
Leaving me scared
They given me a lot
Through so much struggle I have fought
In end I'm left with my pen and pad
The end

The darkness has escaped
Reaching salvation from its great depths
It was and still remains blind
Searching for light
Continuing with sense of hope

Feel my body thump from the grave
As you lay body on mine
Alive he is alive he is not
What you thought reality it came to exist
Alive I am
A spirit amongst the world
My body left to decay
Left my heart and soul to persist
Living amongst the many hearts dreams
I am that brush of wind
That every tingle when alone
That extra warmth at night
That body when needed
Dead oh contraire
For my spirit still breaths today

Scream war
Promote peace
Four five shots
A poster
Relinquish the holds
Break the chains
Kick down the door
Smash the walls
Give up or succeed
Live or die
What do you believe?
One mind one heart
I'm living and going
My soul here and there
My heart is everywhere

How do I begin?
Let me count the ways
Princess with the silver slipper
Awaiting true love at the alter
Hovered over her face white comfort
Causing a jaded vision
Lost and confused
Losing the true essence now shallow
That special abundance of love
Once shared and felt so deep within her core
Those butterflies taken departure
No longer flying without wings
Forced to build a cocoon once again
Never to fly again
Never to find true love again
True love once known
True love now gone

I look and see what is truly meant to be
A simple fatal attraction
I can fulfill your satisfaction
I want to be your simple reaction
I feel what I feel is real
This kiss has never been felt before
Feelings within feel so pure
So deep and rich are your lips
Soft and smooth
Caressing my lips forever more
You're everything I need and know

Coming too close my heart
You've touched me more ways than one
Undoubtedly I love you more and more
Two worlds clinging together
When we kiss the sky opens up
We are everything it needs to be at ease
In fulfilling its every need want and dream
The sky dreams
It's been around never feeling this way
Feelings never to decay or wish to parish
Something heart felt
Something so deep and cherished

The book is like the mind
Similar to culture
So to speak
Make you weak
Sad and cry
Never such a lie
Spit a poetic verse
Meant to curse
Evil, good, and bad
So many implications
Satisfaction and dissatisfaction
Promotions and great deeds
Love and art
Inspiration and salvation and comfort
Respect of self
Perspectives and views
Eyes meant to see
Ears as well to hear

Visualization of self
Meet or crumble
Books speak
Words speak
Food for thought
Sometimes shallow, cold, and resentful
Books are people
People are books
One is mind
The other judge for yourself

Who are you?
Who am I?
Who are you to spy?
My life's no mystery
Seems so hidden
A dark secret
Cast away
MY life's open to views
Ridicule my success
Ridicule my failure
Unhand me forget me
It isn't possible to see
So I say
Who are you?
Who am I?
Open your mind

The world is one
A nation
A country
This planet earth
That can't correspond
Poverty it is
A dollar the case
The streets is war
People hate and deceive
This lifeless world
Motioning for peace
Breaths of love
Life's a gift
Cherish it

Let me die today
Forget tomorrow
6 feet
Ground humbling my acceptance
For I am just another body
Yet a different soul
Lifeless heart
Living soul
Live for the day
Seize the moment
Capture the memories
Wish on a shooting star
Today I lived
Loved and succeeded
For tomorrow is faith
My destiny
Another life to lead
I've lived by no bible
Nor religion
By none reason makes me no different
Simply creative mind
My heart and soul
Depicted decisions

This is an image
This is not an image
So many thoughts running through my mind
So many thoughts undefined
So many thoughts seem confined
So many thoughts defined
So many thoughts concealed
So many thoughts covered
So many thoughts ready to be exposed
So many thoughts of inspiration
Spoken in every word
So many words
So many thoughts
What's the meaning?

Lord in the heavens
Give me wings so I can fly
Fly above soar so high
Above the clouds
Sitting above the world
World at my view
World outside my window
My secret window
Place of confinement
Alone and lonesome
Heaven only knows
The lord only knows
My place of comfort and survival
At one with sense of self
I can be me

She's so self-conscious
Mysterious and strange in so many ways
Such a low self esteem
So much falling down
Her life at a pit
Feeling such pain
So much love at a distance
She remains persistent
Destined to find that sense of harmony
Life full of such hope
Full of such dreams
One day feeling such love
A place where acceptance is a given
Earning is of no importance
Difference is so much similarity
Sense of self is never an issue
Tissue and shoulders are surroundings
Representing the embodiment of what is
What is true and deep and spiritual
Heart felt

So much more to life
So much pain in this game
This game is such a struggle
So hard to eat
Life seems such confinement
Bars holding me back
Within a place of discomfort
So much weary at hand
Only the heaven knows
This life of mine
This life of mind
The life I seem destined
The so many times I seem confined
Each an every my life seems on the line

At the tender age of six I was down
My mind and body and heart and soul down
I was down
I been down
Knowing the individual within
Just another individual
Born but not raised
A part of the math
A statistic in this system
I was true
True to me
True to this is not an image
This is I
Never letting me down
True to my sense of self
Never losing to me

Take a walk with me
In my moment of clarity
Hear what I'm about
I shed these tears
Why I shed these tears
So many fears
What I'm all about
Why I scream and shout
Let this world feel me
Deep down they can't see
So many scars and scabs

Since the first night in it
I swore I would keep it real
Hated by many confronted by so many
Loved by very few

This is my life
Everything in it
Whatever which way they go
I turn the opposite
Committed to wrong direction
Turned the right way

A love forever
So to say
A dreamt dream
A shooting star
So to speak
A wish
You say
Life's beautiful
So I say
Feeling unexplained
Your heart forbids deep emotion
Do the soul says
Soul purpose
Goal in mind
A love forever
So I speak

Things are done
Reality as real as it is
Dreams are dreamt
Existence so real
Emotions are so much within
Feelings are shared
Hearts are broken
Life is real
Death seems never too far
Love seems never meant
Taken for granted
Said within
Said aloud the air to swallow
Amongst the dust and debris
Blowing around
Striking its path
Rain full of such power
Deceit and hurt
No risk for salvation
No shelter
No comfort

Life is a Dream

Life is a dream
Moment in the sky
People dream
Seek god beyond the blue sky
Within the eyes of Christ to be lead
The devil seeks soldiers
In hearts in our minds
A lot of lies
True confessions
Their thoughts and intuitions
Dreams get lost
Sheets seek slaves to hig up on
Hearts bleed
Fatherless children
Motherless child
A child in the dumpster
Through your eyes
This is not your day
This is your life

Soul searching
So destined to find
This true life of mine
Everything that fills my heart and soul within
The love once known
True love once a gift
Love so much cherished
Love so much yearned for
Love once to die for

Deeper than the ocean itself
Beyond heights of the very sky
Seen through the cloudiest sky
Every inch of me
My blood sweat and tears
I pour out every inch of my soul
To hear your very voice
Such warmth to my core

End all rumors and speculations
I did it and I confess to every bit it is
I confess to the serenity of love
Deep within me it seems a constant urge
This feeling seems indescribable
Dreams and fantasy occur rapidly
Constant repeated reminders
Thoughts racing
Feelings of such urge chasing
Fast enough for my imagination to capture
Soul left not to capture
Without further a due
I love you

I'm from the streets
The streets raised me
I've become immune to it
Never been baptized
Believed to have caught a spirit at least three or four times
People continue that same rhyme
Every day and every week

This is I
The image you see
God given mixed with so much
Dirt on my hands
Not an angel heaven sent
A being like so many that walks
Just another individual

An inspiration I am
An instrument with a voice
Here for a reason
Exploring my soul in this globe
In search of that vibration
An abundance of dedication
A rose in concrete
A card in a full house
One being
One voice
One mind
Let me be heard

I stepped on your porch
I stepped on your paws
Fist fighting we continued
I love you to this day
Through hell and fire
We still remain thick through trying times
We walked the red stop lines and yellow lines
So many goals in mind
So much on our mind
So much to attain
So much remained unsettled
He left a void
Footprints all over
We spoke his name in vain
Left so much to gain
His loss
White powder seemed so important
White over black
The feans made him
We made each other

After my departure
Let me rest and be weary
Do not shed a tear
For I am not out in the cold
Nor am I left astray
I stand beside our lord savior Jesus Christ
I am with his son
Far not from you
So close within your heart
My soul rests
My spirit forever lives on
Let me die at peace to mind

Let my soul never be distorted
Always remembered
Never spoke down upon
Spit to a disgrace
Never lost in space
For I will be remembered
For all that is good and prosperous
All that is longevity
Forever living in the hearts and memories

Liberty has no name
Refrain from identity
Liberty speaks as does her soft lips
Such a soft spoken voice
Love speaks as well her heart
Soul speaks as if crashing waves
Her heartbeat sends shivers
Mental thoughts make my soul quiver
Such dreams seem never impossible
I can fly
I can fly

The bridge
The, the, the bridge
I claim lay to
My resting spot
I've earned my respect at home
The red stop signs and yellow lights
I walked through night and day
Pen and pad in my hand
Where I've scoped this gracious land
Land of hopes and dreams
Destined to capture
Wherever whoever I lay eyes upon
My eyes on the prize
So much seems disguised
I can't hide forever
I must get out
I must come up

It appears so clear
Though life seems so severe
I seem like prey
But feel as though I'm a predator
Defying not death itself
In fact the odds against me
I shed that same blood
I bleed with tears
Showering upon me
Feeling every drop
Ceasing in my own pool of tears
Blood sweat and tears I've cried
My life appears in my hand
As well so much others
Taken at any given time
A split second can be
Another millisecond eternal sleep

Let me justify myself
What more can I say
In my moment of clarity
I know what girls like
Where I'm from
My first song
The upbringing
I've had a million and one questions
The city is mine
Friend or foe if so if not
You'll always be my sunshine
Threats and 99 problems
I've changed my cloths
Brushing my dirt off my broad shoulders
While the streets were watching
I've just begun to rhyme
You must love me

I have so much on my plate
I breathe the hunger for no more
I've met my appetite
Quenched my deepest thirst
My heart beats so fast
My soul rumbles amongst my mind
Making no sense it appears
Not knowing what's next
Feeling the deepest of dreams haunt me
Solidifying its dominance
It appears to take control of reality
I have not the courage to walk
Not the mind to seek
It is it could be
Reality seems imagination
Life seems a distant dream
Life seems a mile away

Life appears pointless
Death seems evident
It's eminent I'm going to die
Life seems as though a grave shift
I can't fathom life without a struggle
Life without this hustle
My pen and pad
Appears the only thing I have
Inking then to my prime
Yet to hit my prime
It's just begun
Having so much to say
What more can I say
So much on my mind
So much to mine
They will feel me
This is god given
Freedom to mind
Freedom of mine

Not known for blasting my chrome
Nor surpassing my own
Threats don't impress me
How dare you wish death upon me
I see the envy
You lust what I possess
You lust what I access
I've been oppressed
Straight from my umbilical cord
Through the wire
I walked I ran
I took my stand
I been a savage
I been afraid
I been in that cage
I walked on fire
I've drowned
I've blown the bubbles
Felt the cold air
I've shed tears of fear
I've vacated so much
I've been personified
I've been identified
Been condemned
Time to extend
Thanks an praise
Lord and savior Jesus Christ

I feel like I can't vent into words
I struggle to fight
I struggle to breath
My existence seems faded
Drifting away from the importance
True essence of life itself
True essence of mine
I love you too much to lose you
Your spiritual deepness
I know it may slip away
The way it use to be
The way it could be
The eyes in which I could see
Direction I was headed in
Detours along the way
People and destinations I wish to stay

Pictures are not for the wall
They remain a vivid thought
They remain not shaded
They remain not tainted
They remain not a memory
They remain a memory
Never making sense
But what you make of it
Life makes sense
Life makes not complete sense
Feel me
As matter a fact still feel me

I can't find what makes me strong
Rejuvenating my true heart
I once was he
I once loved her

I still love her so deep
My core deep within
The love to write
I cannot find again
I put my heart into it
I cannot no more
Maybe I am now
Maybe I did then
I know the reason no more
True purpose eludes me
Finding its way back
I don't know it's the hate frustration or hunger
Finding me to vent this
Life seems so pitiful
I Find it hard to get through these stain tears
Feel me
Still feel me

I am the leader
The general of the opportunist
He who fears death is in-denial
By your side
Along the way
To lead you not astray
Two thumbs
Eight fingers
Somewhere they're to linger with
Show you the hope and praise
The answers are plenty
By your side
By my side
Together as one

Darkness placates the city full of such bright light
Red stop signs and yellow lines
Love fills the air
Such places to go
Such a person to seek
Behind some door
Hidden amongst the shadows
Open such a mind not oblivious to love
Such a pain cannot be felt
Tears that bleed
Flooding the very streets
You cannot feel this love amongst the clouds
Deeper than the very sky itself
Pain no more
Love seeks such a shallow to find
In the mist of this very life

The truth and true ties
To that I testify
To every word written
To every word I spewed
It is I
It is I
I was gone and lost her
Explaining who I was
How I lost me
The critics rave
Deep down they love me
Offence taken
I had no remorse
Though some hatred with a need to vent
I aired it out
I swore to be real
In that I revealed
No periods airing it out
Opening it up by flipping the script
I was I
I am I was again
Not jaded with a need to break barriers
This could be my first and last log fire
I love you
If you love me
I hope to inspire
Refraining from holding back
Having so much to say
This love of mine that elaborates so fluently
Spitting this lisp of conscious
Words of wisdom for there wealth
Stressing the message to the unknown
The message unknown

For what its worth
Take it
I made my choices
Feel me
Still feel me

Across the island
Separated by a beautiful body of water
She lies on the beach
My love and life
My earth, moon, and stars
Unforgettable such a soul
Such a beauty
Waves crash, as does her mind
I'm on her mind
I am her mind as well is mine
She is mind and mine
I sit adjacent to her
Grasping the sand
Steering steep into her
Wondering dreaming
Mind at a daze
Nothing in particular
Love is this beautiful
Life is this beautiful
I've awakened this is not a dream
Reality as it may
Is mind and mine
I love you

They must have Forgot

I haven't been around the world. Hell, I can top that, and I have yet to grace the air on a plane. I cleaned the inside of a glock nine; big brother did his time, and just touched down. We touched base the minute he touched. I waited at the station, love is love. Even after the dusks clear, I still will ride this one out to the death of me. Tonya is still around forever around and around forever. I continue to play with the wordplay; creating something that no one can ever grasp the concept of. I want to be a trendsetter, raising the bar to new limits for those around me to reach or even over topple. I'm from the city where kids pick up flags and represent their set. The way things are transpiring it looks like they might have a cell for me. I'm trying to make it in an imperfect world; where the guns have more value than books. City hall is worried about a train system, chairs, or who should be elected. Important yet, has anyone displayed their value or has their word meant anything these days? Why should I be taken seriously? Must I repeat myself when I say I have more balls than everyone put together in city hall? Quote me please.

I'm not going to be the one to criticize a system based on belief. Instead, I can just continue to state reality and what has been going on in a system run by people unqualified. We go to war for the actions of individuals; while the students in the school system fight for a flag they were brought up on. Wrong? That's not the case but we were taught to fight for what we believe in—whether it is for oil, Osama, or whatever the case. The homeless fight over bread and what side of the street they want to be on, because of what it means to them. In return I pose the question what is really important anymore? What is of significance? Are my words of significance? My heart continues to write for a cause that no one can see; much less believe, and failing to be heard because I have yet to sign a major publishing deal, though it has been my dream. I'm not sure if that's important anymore, due to the respect I get these days. I'm not a rapper, nor do I spit the better lines, nor am I rich, my lines however are so rich I could feed Africa and then some. I'm confident on another level to which I can surpass the best of them. Jim Carrol is by far one of the best to grace the stage but I'm trying to create a bigger supremacy than he ever had, though I respect everything that is anything he has ever done. Nonetheless, I have to become something monumental.

Still Here

I'm still here doing the thing that matters to me most. I never taught myself, it seems I just figured out how to put my heart into something that matters to me most. I don't know whether to blast off at a few individuals, or creatively reconstruct the individual that has now graced you with his words in "Far from Home". I don't know where it was taking me, whether I was free of the constraints that had me uplifted, or to justify that love that still eludes me to this very day. I've been blessed with such honour and prestige to be in love with such beauties that still remain in the back of my mind. I've learned a lot over the past few years; kissing beautiful girls, converting with such educated geniuses, been through so much, which so many of you have learnt about over the past few years.

My life is more than what it seems. It can be whatever you want it to be, whether it be a black tunnel, or sunny on a beautiful Sunday morning. "Far from Home" is here, delivered to everyone in the mail. It's time for me to move on from that though it remains in the back of my mind, a love so precious.

I've been fortunate enough to let my life breathe the way I have stressed it. My family, far from home. The many individuals who have surrounded over time, and that lost love that walked away into pitch dark. I've experienced a great degree throughout my quest for life itself, as I only know. I live my life not according to others or the sky that seems that it has destiny within it. It's simply something that never ends in my mind, I want to see beyond it because beauty is in the eye of the beholder, and I see that now in regards to life.

There's a message in my words, you have to decode it to the best of your ability. I'm standing at the bottom of the map; I have yet to see to beauty of my city, as well as my world, let alone what it has to offer me. I hear Italy is a sight to see.

This love of mine seems to elude me still. After such a long period of time, I still find myself wanting to empty out my thoughts and dreams to you, love. Time has passed; we have grown beyond ourselves so long ago. I still live there dreaming about your beautiful appearance that used to grace me, but now it is only in my dreams. God bless your baby boy once again, you don't need advice but live for him like you lived for us, and can't anybody hold him down. I have too many soft-spoken words for you my love. I've cleared my agendas, wrote a book about your love, I've uttered my thoughts, become someone I knew along time ago, and still am to this very day. Truth is, I think I know what it takes to make you happy; but really I have no clue. All I can do is dream and that's all I've done of you, love. It's been long enough, love, to see your face all I hold is a picture of us in my dreams and it's killing me. I can't even be graced with your very existence, yet you're just a phone call away, and just a bus ride down the block.

I heard Mary sing and I thought to myself I had to speak to you again—not physically but through words—not hoping you know how I feel, but to get a lot off my chest that has plagued my mind for quite some time.

I sit here, tea in hand, such a common thing for me. Snowflakes are trickling down, brushing everything in their path, so soft and kind, lady-like. I'm caught at a pause once again, reminiscing way too much into a love that once was, and appears never to attach to me again. I stand with happiness in my heart for you, but I fail to be at peace with us. I don't know whether it is because a lot was left unsaid; my heart stays forbidden to say so much, however I find peace of mind. State my heart onto a paper that never talks back, just reiterates what I fail to utter to your heart. Looking in your beautiful eyes, mine appear to be a leaky faucet, as I begin to imagine myself uttering just the words "I love you." I become complacent with thoughts of you. I am filled with so many thoughts of what if my life hadn't went down the way it did, if you didn't fall out of place through life's tractable road that seem paved for the both of us, not left to follow. I feel like you were a miracle that I believed in so much. I was not one to believe in too much until my eyes were placed upon you, miss. You're the one who told me to believe that these miracles were real, your very words were to zone out with you and let myself go, and be free for a while nature took its place. Love followed behind us and guided us every step of the way.

We were destined to be something close to greatness, if not that. We were simply something special. I paint a vivid picture of how we would look together today, while you are away in my heart rocking your son to sleep. I pray for your first child and every success that he endeavors. God bless the child. I want to say so much, so I ask of your acceptance while I write the letters, as I make vivid sense of what has taken place in your absence. They say I have become a miracle. I say yes. They say the kid is a writer in the making, something special. I say no. I disagree with a lot of accusations. A couple of things are for sure, I have been declared a king, and sometimes ignorant they say. I try to be modest and humble but it's like they won't accept it, they keep pulling me back in. I have no choice but to take all that comes and deals with it; as long as they never take my pen and pad away. I remain shackled with these chains, with thoughts and visions just to dream but never to come true. Reason being, I have not an ounce of control over, but let my words speak for themselves. If you're going to feel me, then you're going to feel me. That's that, I have not a pinch of control over that either, my words however speak for themselves so listen and pay close attention. So many things have been going on. Walk with me.

Love stays vacant in the back of my mind while I await your ghostly image. I wish you could feel me, the way I cried after such a long period of time since you've been gone. I feel like I love you more than life itself at times, because you remain in my mind more than I think about my own Goddamn soul. You I want more than life itself. I feel bold making these statements, to be real. These appear to be just the facts because when you have fallen in love the way I have, there's not much to envision or imagine more than perfection itself. A lot of people are going to be offended at a lot of the things that I am saying, but to be real that's I can do is give you and my surroundings the truth.

Where I'm going

I got my mind made up, my back to the wall; my homies want to bang the streets squeezing every little bit because they were taught that every little bit counts. I have a lot of beliefs; at times it becomes difficult to believe in a lot that has been said to me. On the other side of things, I have always felt like I have made my own rules because they left me very young, and that sperm donor never stopped to think about that egg that hatched in that woman's womb. It's okay, I'm here. He's old news. Enough of that saga, onto bigger and better things.

I wish my homies could see that this fast life is not the way to go. Cops try to keep them confined, is the belief, but the truth is that it is all in the mind. Even the people behind bars have dreams beyond their confinement, and dreams that they weren't in this position. Life forever changes; drive-bys occur, life changes in an instant. I don't know why I write these words. At times I like to think I do, but when I think about it, it's my love for the world and the movement I want to create for everyone to follow. I was a leader before they even thought I could be, I was a son before I was born. In all honesty I am the golden child because these superiors thought I didn't have it within me to get up out the struggle. Honestly I haven't, because I have left a lot behind. Among them all, a lost love forever that still plagues my mind to this very day. I saw the tears of a mother when she lost her son; I received that phone call when my uncle was paralyzed. I dropped to my knees, the floor in agony and pain. For a second I was in his position and it hurt. I saw a soldier die last year, he was shot three times. Three things he had were a heart, pain, and the will to take his family to greater limits by any means. Needless to say he made his choices and he lived with it and I hope God understands his grief and pain. I've always been like heat on the thermostat; always rise to the top of all else.

My life is taking me to a lot of places to which I haven't a vivid thought of where I want to even be. These girls proclaiming that they love me after such a short period of time. I don't know what to think anymore. Wondering what world they live in, and if I am what they truly believe I am. Am I a diamond amongst this fake gold? What is it they truly see? I know what it is I'm looking for, but I haven't found the thing remotely close to that. I've tasted love and the bittersweet taste of defeat. I have the hunger for more, but it scares me too much to get attached to something. I don't know whether to believe I am insecure in my thoughts or feelings; whatever the case, it's been hard to cope through tears because anyone who has sworn to be down in my heart has left a trail of no return. I anxiously hold onto memories that I have had, dreams that I once thought of, that are now of no significance.

I have thoughts of you not knowing how to love me the slightest little bit. Love for me is something truly deep and spiritual that I share beyond comparison to anything you can name. I have tasted it, felt it touch my heart, touch my core before my soul; and above all else it has never left me lonely. You, for one, have never meant any harm toward me, you have this belief that you were built to love to me, but truly you have no idea how to love me, and that is okay. I'm saying you should love me; I want to be your homie, your best friend, your companion, and most importantly, your everything.

You lost the true essence of a kiss, a hold on me that you use to have, your way to keep me enticed by someone as beautiful as you inside and out. I want to kiss you every moment of the day, I want to hold you and tell you I love you a million times a day. I want you to know that you are above all else that matters in life to me. You are truly something precious that I attempt to describe. Every day I awake to the very beautiful thought of you. I think of you as I drink my hot tea in the morning, as I sweeten it, knowing nothing can be as sweet as you. Milk makes my tea a bit bitter and you, on the other hand, can never be bitter. I can taste you from a mile away, the very thought of you warms my heart and quenches my thirst. You have no idea what you mean to me, my queen. My love never lies. Love takes time, and energy, though at times it is consuming, but nonetheless, it stands amongst us as something that is truly unique. I don't want to teach you how to love me because that's not what it's about. It's about knowing, feeling and connecting with that person.

Hear Me

So-called friends are being scandalous to this very point, saying one thing then doing another. Caught in that jealous triangle, no need to be. She's always going to be there for me whether you like it or not. If you can't stand the heat then get up out of the kitchen. I can be blatant and ignorant but that's up to you to decide whether I am or not. Needless to say, let's be real. Don't ever try to come at me with that Mickey Mouse story, I'm not about that. Just stick to waking with it in your mouth; that alone should be your only concern.

They say I've gone off into this new world, vanishing into this deep emotion hating and forgetting about the most important things about life and more importantly, family. I haven't forgotten. I just needed time to reflect on my life and the way things were going; all the wrongs and rights that have plagued me over such a long period of time. Since "Far from Home" I haven't had time to sit down and think about the many things in my life that are taking place. A lot of you don't know how things go down. It's not as easy as 1, 2, 3 these days. My parents have no control. Then again, they never did. Nonetheless, I have to make plans and decisions on my own. That's not how I get down, and that's not how I ever got down with it. I'm not gone, I just went down the street away from home, so I can put myself out there and do so many of the things that I was put on this soil to do. They say it's God's plan but I'm not religious nor will I ever be for that matter, no disrespect to God. I put the spotlight on my life for a minute or two. My brother was confined for such a period of time, and since he's been in, it's been too much to bear. The other was missing him, looking for a role model to look up to, and watch over him because I was not taking that place. I was out running the streets, trying to grab a bite to eat and exploring this city that I haven't seen the outer doors of. I haven't been on the plane yet, ever to Spain, Jamaica, Italy, not tasting wine in France. I have no idea what this world has to offer, except downtown in the city that never sleeps.

I never meant any harm. I love you, it's just that this world is such a cold place and I know that's what you were thinking and still think to this day; but your big brother has never left. You went under the guidance and tutelage of the many that surround you like fake brothers that had your back. I ran it all day every day; push or shove I was always there. He's out now. I just wish you would see the true beauty of us all together as one, we know who her best friend is, but we could still do it. She's still that same beautiful queen that gave birth to us and loves us so much but continues to constitute the many things that are going on, never failing to substitute love for her best friend. I love her through thick and thin despite the pain she put me through.

He did a lot in front of my eyes, many of the things you were too young to see but became clearer at a later age. I will never forgive him for doing the many things he did, dumping her head in and out of the water. It's a scary thought. There were so many kids around; and I know we don't know that man anymore because he has grown so much over the past years. He left for a while in an attempt to find his true self and purpose in life. He accomplished that and more. The man we saw before him was not the man that held me at birth, rocked me to sleep and told me the real dude was not around so he would accept ownership to the crown.

I'm an egg who just happened to hatch that no one ever wanted including the elderly one whose intention was never to watch over my life and play a significant part in it. However, I was born through it all, a mouth, a big lip, and big head, that refuses to stop refining myself into the man that no one could ever imagine; fighting for everything that was right and nothing that was wrong. I never knew the bastard. He appeared not in my rearview. I heard his voice twice claiming to be the one, I only knew that there was just one and that was not him. The tailor did a lot of harm and I'll never forgive him; but through thick and thin he fought not only for what he believed in, but also for kids that were not his.

She lost it at some point that I can't recall. A few friends showed her a good time and that was that, I vaguely recall. She believed in so much, miracles, as she sent us off to church every Sunday morning. I still remember those days waking up, watching wrestling and her preparing us to meet the lord in His house. She always told us that God had a plan and we were a part of it. I was a blessing in disguise in her eyes; a child, one of two, born by an accident so some say, but what can I say about it? I'm here now, alive and well, breathing in the confusion of the air they call home.

A lot of people have been talking about me, and everywhere I am, running their mouths about and reverberating a lot of things that have reached my eardrums. I feel the need to creatively construct what has transpired since the last time I saw a lot of individuals. One thing's for sure, I don't care how any of you take what was said or is about to be said; it's real talk, street talk, and too many people are like birds chirping on a Sunday morning.

My condolences to Wilson strip, we walked under the bridge every day. I created my surroundings when the jungle click disappeared because they refused to fight for their own brothers. They weren't real at the time. I left them, a few refused to follow in my footsteps. I then went on to create a circle of individuals I fail to mention because if I get at you, it won't be fair. It's just a fight you won't win, believe me. I was in control, the leader in every aspect. It wasn't what I said, but more or less what I did, creating a movement for everyone to follow so we can all be successful in the process. A few individuals got selfish and decided to go beyond their boundaries and create tension with me. It was dealt with when I threatened to kick you to the curb and told you that this click was never you, slitting your wrist when I was there for you; and on the other side of things recording a poem in the paper on me, taking subliminal shots. It's okay though, good thing you looked at your watch and thought for a brief second, luckily you know what time it was before you did what you thought you could have done.

To the dude still whacking off in front of my computer screen, we all know that you're still at it. Continue to do that job because apparently you do a bang-up job. God bless your newborn child, I heard the news, and I'm ecstatic. You having a kid even barely knowing how to take care of yourself.

Make no mistake, I'm not bitter nor am I sounding off or trying to fire the first blow. It's something that's been on my mind for quite sometime. I wrote with no fear like I continue to do everyday so with that said who cares that I offend. For that matter, I may even offend the president in the White House, maybe even the people in the seats at City Hall but truth be told (and I'll put it blatantly and as clear as possible) I have more balls than everyone put together in the White House and City Hall. Please quote me on that. I could care less.

Short but Sweet

At this point in time, I lie in a bed of confusion with roses that you cannot stand the smell of, and cannot stand the sight. I remain consumed with your happiness, your smile that has me caught in this web of laughter and smiles of joy. Every thought of you has me wanting you in so many ways that I can't even imagine, I don't know what it is that has me so tangled within this sea, this web of confusion, cause no matter how many times I get out I find myself falling right back in. This sea of confusion, crashing waves, I hit rock after rock, shore after shore, taste of different sand, so many different people, so many surfers, different styles, so many colors, so many thoughts as the sun turns to different shades, so many different directions, the earth is still revolving and turning as we speak. I don't know whether I'm at a standstill in my life, or if I'm just lost within this difficult thing they call love. I've been there before, a long time ago, but also what appears to be a short time ago.

I'm Back

Break out the red carpet, open your doors, and tell her I'm back with a vengeance. This is not easy to say, so I'll try to make as much sense as I can. You don't know me, so let me give you a bit of insight into who it is I really am, as I try to make sense of what it is I am trying to accomplish. The count is, a lot are being shot down, and it started when I was at the age of fourteen, and no I didn't lose it to her. I decided that everyone was assuming the obvious, so I went and ran with it. To no extent did I think it would turn out like this, still heart-wrenched for her, I miss you love. I'm sorry I said what I said. It wasn't a mistake though; it was something that needed to be done so doesn't take any offence to it. What was said about what took place, it's all said and done for a reason and one day when you sit down and think about it you will figure it out.

At this point in time, word is you're reading "Far from Home", what a piece put together by yours truly. There were a lot of heartfelt moments that I had in mind, which I try to recall every time I pick up my pen and pad, as I try to carve some type of image from the past that continues to elude me to this very day. It's time that I tell you what I haven't told you, even though I feel like I have told you everything that happened. I find myself constantly thinking about a lot of things, stuff that I left out of the very story itself, as well things that I still feel. At times I get repetitive, boring.

I remain consistent in the search of the very definition of love itself, the constant feel of it, its texture, the many gestures, every thought, every feel, the feeling deep within my stomach, as it twirls in constant motion. The love that I make to it, if ever I get to that position which was once a dream that I had with you, and for you. Truth is, I find myself journeying off into planets unheard of or even remotely discussed between individuals. It was so long ago but I saw it and still see it to this very day. I have seen it since then, however, I get caught up emotionally within the depths of the feeling itself. Never losing concentration, but pain that has followed me throughout my life won't allow me to cross the very river of salvation that enables me to be free from all constraints, the thoughts and dreams that I once had with you. I can look past you more and more each day as the hours, minutes, and seconds, even milliseconds cross and tick away. I've fallen so deep that no one in their right mind can pick me up, your thoughts and dreams have me weak to a point of no return or so I think when the very thought of you arises.

The reward from this journey itself is something I long for. The walk is long the road not paved; never forgetting the past, the pain, lost friends, the rain. Family they say is thick. I fail to judge the critics themselves and no longer do they speak. Hear my words. Listen to me. Speak my words. I'm something special never to be forgotten. Far from Home, next up Inhaled Silence. No barriers no constraints. Still riding down for the love and the appreciation life is offering, never forgetting my roots.

I'm sitting back in the revolving chair trying to make sense out of emotion, and the madness that is taking place at this particular time. The friends who think life is a competition, the other ones who think they were cool and everything is so-called gravy. I've got to laugh at times but to be honest my skin is only so thick.

Things have changed

A lot has changed. I think I have found the answer to all my problems but in reality I have no clue where I am in life, so I cannot come to a conclusion just yet. A lot of people are not respecting the loyalty I have toward them. Don't get it twisted. I'm not trying to create enemies but let me let the world and the people who are surrounding me know the truth about where I stand at this point. I wrote my first book sometime ago, I said a lot of names just to be real because I had an abundance of respect for a lot of the people that help mould me and in that I meant help feed into the fire that helped burn into God's son that has blessed you with his words.

He made his video straight out of the slums out of the hood, the jungle city. I'm a rose that grew from concrete. He never represented me or the story that took place. What happened to circle B, under the bridge, the two that died and they built the legendary court on which they hold yearly basketball games? Let it be known this is not a beef movement whether I shout your name out, keep it real or leave it alone, real talk. My main concern these days is writing in my diary every day. I want people to feel the fire that burns within. My uncle was paralyzed and I felt the pain but not his, it was mine saying he missed so much, it's eating him up inside cause he needs me more than ever. His best friend died drinking and driving, and my significant other is still at the bottle, and others are following in her footsteps. Shy Brat is balling out the last chance at success in Daytona; my brothers are still alive trying to live each day, day by day.

I took the name, put it on my back with my bare hands. It's not what I'm looking to carry but I don't have a choice at this point in my life. I sat in the offices, expressed my thoughts, solidifying my every opinion whether they respected it or not. Call me the underdog, whatever it is; whatever is your desire. Just when you thought it was fists to cuffs now I have fighting words to blaze back. If you had grasped the concept from my last piece, I have always been imbedded with my own perception, respecting your conception. I awake every morning respectful of all that there is to be for me, as well as the burning hunger within my core, to want more with my life. I feel the breath of hatred but I continue the flow of love to this beat that I roll to running through all my veins.

I'm not one of the six men who lifted the flag back in 1945, so I guess I'm not of significance. I have to create my own significance. On March 12, 2006 I blessed the world with my words in "Far from Home". In return, the phone calls, the accusations and the messages started to build. I crossed barriers and disrespected my people on a number of levels. In all respect I meant no harm but it's quite clear I got your attention and that was my main intention.

I don't need to sell for me to be happy. It's not a competition. If it were, I would take a few shots and let it be known I was here to win. I want my hood, my people to feel my words and understand why I awake to my words and conscious every morning by letting you all know that we are directed by choice in life, so I direct my energy toward my opposition. I wrote it for so many reasons. I needed to release what was on my mind for quite some time. I flew away into the sunset, as did my first love. What was the past is now my distant future; it's all now behind me. I'm hopeless in this attempt as I try to draw on the beauty of life itself; in that I see the beauty in everything that I lay eyes on or even have the slightest clue about.

I live in an imperfect world where my surroundings appear to be perfect yet we all have flaws. I'm far from perfect, but I'm more than the average Joe, better than that sperm donor, better than a bottle of liquor, and I'm welcoming all the shooters cause it's not a problem for me these days. I'm above all else trying to earn the respect of the rich, sign book deals, not selling myself short. Nonetheless my words are being sold for the almighty in life, dollars. I have no intentions to hit a million though I'm sure that would be something special. I want to be back in Hamilton playing checkers with the man who never left my side, I want the mother I knew sometime ago, I miss you.

I have no choice but to do this fight on my own, choosing my own words, cause this is not a hobby as it once was, it's a reality where I live everyday. I want the world to feed off history that I am beginning to create. I'm not waiting on offers for the diary, just your eyes and ears, pay close attention. Feel my harsh words, but I'm not a critic at all, just a philosopher to some extent. Music is food to my soul as I continue to grow. I'm getting a little sensitive these days; they ask why I'm so defensive. It's because I take a lot of offensive because every death affects me, murder rate, and the drugs that continue to pollute the streets that raised me. I know a few doing life bids, I don't want to visit Paul's grave cause it's not my place; he's up above and if he respects that then there should not be an issue. I'm not celebrating his death these days. He was a beautiful person, and he wants me to do what I'm doing, so the respect is there. I heard your mother passed a few days ago, sorry for your loss. I never knew the lady but I heard great things. I prayed for her the same day she lay in the hospital but I never visited the cemetery where she lays. With all due respect, that was not my place, at the end of the day, I know who my true friends are, and where they stand when the moon begins to fall. I fell off for a year. I had to attend to business after everyone rolled on to his or her own life, and I never got bitter. I returned and it was like I was never gone. The phone calls stopped coming from the other end of the phone. Nothing. A ghost. Where were you? I was out on my grind while you picked up the books, so much to accomplish as I continued to earn my place. The words of encouragement I never heard, on the other hand I never asked for much. I heard the rumors, I would have returned in my own fashion, and once again that wasn't my place. You must have lost your mind, clowns; this is definitely not a fight, or a verbal confrontation you can step to, so fast forward to silence. Make no mistake about it when I return. I heard you loud and clear, you left your fingerprints all over, so get up out of the chair you sat in all year and let's see what's next.

I sat back and asked myself how is this possible? You let the blood flow through your veins and let that anger and frustration drive you to say so many things that took shots at my character. It's a loss; lost situation cause the real people who know me, know that it wasn't where I stand. For you to even have those thoughts is utterly ridiculous. I have a front row seat when I get back cause I want to see your facial expressions. I have nothing to prove to the few who think I have time to waste over senseless issues; but it needed to be addressed.

Letter to my City

Few words can describe how much I miss my city; they named it back in the early nineties: Jungle City. I miss hanging out at the circle, under the bridge, and the fights in the schoolyard. My brother they say snitched, and though a lot of you did I'm not mad, I still love my homey. I live outside my city; but word gets around because I'm just a phone call away. The wars are brewing like coffee at Tim Horton's every morning; consistent. A soldier died last summer, his kids left without a father. I used to run on the road with him to different schools. He was a comedian but he loved life, he accepted what he had no control over and I respected him for that. I can respect a man who wants to be something even though it hurts. I can respect a man who tries to make something of himself from the depths of nothing. If I'm not mistaken your mother used to blaze you a blunt. She wasn't scared of anything, the streets are where she was from, and it's where we all grew up. I'm a product of my environment. I am the streets.

I learned how to be a man through each and every one of you. I'm a man now and I can admit most men don't know how to be a man these days. I never walked away from that little one who sat in her womb. She decided she didn't want to have a little one running around at the time. She made the choice not to have the child. A lot of people believed that I left the city; truth is it's still on my back, as I speak through my words. I see the little girls running around the city having kids; kids having kids, at such a young age. I can't sit around and watch this go on. So many people are digging my spirit; truth be told most beautiful girls are not ready to embrace me with such love. Though many speak of love, they do not know about it. Truth is, my love lies a lot deeper than you know. I want to raise the many kids but I have not the power to do so. When I speak it's unique; I'm not trying to be a writer, they say I am, if so, let it be. I awake to my diary every morning as I try to create these vivid memories. I think back to my past, running to Scarborough claiming our sets, going through the Jewish area, taking bikes, fighting. Doing whatever to it took to attain more in life, by any means necessary.

Making sure lunch money was provided for all of us the next morning for school; running to the chocolate bus in time 'cause a handful of money was waiting. A donation in my pocket was the most important thing during those days when no one was providing for me. I'm a soldier in my eyes, no matter how you cut it up and cook it. I was raised through crack, weed, and warfare; I wouldn't have it any other way because that is not what they predicted. Some of my homeboys are dead, but I'm still alive to tell the many stories. Peanut butter and jam sandwiches after basketball games with my brother, walking through the cold, having a snowball fight, and running from twisted realities. So young and trying to live, Fox died, shoot-outs and fist fights are what I watched. My mother raised me through thick and thin, and I thank her for that despite what went on. Without her, I would not be here.

A few of you are not representing your set to the fullest extent; I must admit I'm quite appalled. When you see whatever, whomever, and me if you've got an issue, I'll be more than happy to take that up with you wherever. A lot of people have asked me why I'm so mad—but it's a matter of principles: respect, integrity and loyalty, which few people see these days. I remain loyal to my roots to the very depths of my core. I respect my people and even the strangers that surround me on the transportation system each day. I see so much in people, the beauty of it all. I walk through my city, I see the kids, the parents. What's wrong with the school system? Everything, The parents, the teachers, no initiative, it's not a job anymore, it's your life. When you signed the deal you told yourself you wanted to create change, or least that's what you thought. I'm not trying to preach because that is not my place in this world, but I command the respect of you listening to my every word because I will be heard.

My words are proclaimed from the first word written down to every sentence forth. This is about my city and me, my boys, whether they accept me or not or if they ever did, and the girls who pretended to love me for me. I refuse to sell my soul or a few words for that matter. I want more out of everyone in this world. The soul's purpose is for everyone to see the beauty within, so they can move on in life. If they can accept themselves, they can they project themselves to do more. Build the courage to want to see more, do more, and witness success. As I put pieces together I try to innovate myself as an individual, I'm moulding myself into a greater man than I ever was and ever will be. I'm one of the most real, still alive; my word means everything to me. It's all I have, the code of the streets; it's what we live by. The ones who gave their word sold out, many fail in their existence. I'm not your cousin, it was a lie to get by, you never liked me, and you never will. As you sit back and smoke your spliff, know that I'm in the office on my grind, penning this book while you attempt to make it in the little thing you call a home. You need me, come find me. Better yet, I might be at the circle hanging it with the people you call a crew, so come find me. The new voice of the city, they say he's the one rapping so his voice is being heard. Far from Home is on the shelf about to go brick. The bricks fall and so do your sales, I'm checking your sound scan, and to be honest I'm not that impressed. Tell the streets who you really are, you're selling your soul for a measly buck, I'm way too real. For the record, the rhythm and blues is not working. Get another job. As for me, I'm the one who is out there on the grind, so keep my name out of your mouth.

Drop all the excuses, I picked up the purpose and ran with it. I await the planes to Europe but I stand in my supremacy, where I rule my own domain. Never too much to rule these days, doesn't really mean much. I need no crown to stake claim to the city. Whether I'm at circle B, or over the bridge, it's still my city. I don't care if he's rapping, he knows nothing that's going on. There is a history; however, he knows not his journey or the way we came about, red stop signs and yellow lines. We see it on every corner, I still hear the gunshots, yeah Fox died. Fox died, I was reborn. I heard the stories, the rumors, and the deals that were made, but I had my thoughts and with that the roads I have paved.

I have learned to make a man out of myself. Things seem to transpire but so does life; changes are thrown my way—obstacles, tests that I face, it's all a matter of life. Matter I can overcome. I consider myself a breath of fresh air because of the words I choose to represent myself. I am different in every way; my thoughts are beyond my prime.

True Friends

Thank God for granting me this moment of clarity, so you could all hear my truth. I promised I would keep to myself and not open my mouth, but I hear it loud and clear. You left your fingerprints, so you had to be there. I didn't make it to the site, I wasn't present. True friend, I think not; but you're welcome to uphold your views as well as your opinions about life. We make our own decisions and we live with them. I don't need to clarify myself, but that would just be ignorant of me not to. We all have to uphold an image, maintain that we are hard, when in fact we are not. We're soft at heart. I could sit here and send out a few shots at a couple people and it would be easy for me to do so. Unless you want to respond in a negative way, then I will put your shit to rest so don't fuck with me. Take it how you want to take it. That is not what this is about. It's about friends that were friends, having our friendships, some not respecting others.

I'm not trying to create enemies with it, but true friendship was never there, never real. I left for a whole year. I never heard a phone call; he said she said shit, it's all a load of shit. I'm too real for fucking words. It hurts to know that someone I know lost someone. Vent all you want, but take a look back at life and think about it logically, who really is your friend these days? When I fell were you there to pick me up? I was left out in the cold and I needed your jacket to keep me warm, were you there? It's not about that, it's about your circle and who you roll with. We all had a different type of friendship toward each other; a few didn't like what others had to say. A lot of things were said with some playing their role to an extent. Nonetheless, we are all human so look deep within yourselves and think about what's more important in life. Creating bitter enemies or making eminence with the ones who we have fought with for so long? You lost her, but you haven't learned anything from it, or so it appears. I'm not taking shots at you, I am merely saying you're about doing what you have to do; in the clubs, all your friends, and the ones that have been there and really do know you. I thought to myself, why not respond to this note, because I am a part of it, whether you think I am or not. I love the dude I know what he's about, I love you I know what you're about, and nonetheless we dig holes that we cannot get out of. We brew wars, restart shit from the past, we stoop to new levels. New year, new breed, new life, three kings. I still role with, homegirl Tonya's still here. She tells me keep hope alive in her own way, the love is here. I'm out here on the fucking grind. My nigga just passed last summer I didn't attend the funeral, respect is due, and for you respect was due.

After death you think we would have learned to look past our biased views and be the bigger person, but we are all guilty of this. I read the notes, so I wrote my note. Never made the phone call, I sent the messages, and I was heard loud and clear. I didn't expect a response, just letting you know how I felt. Whether I see you embrace me or shun me, truth is we all have a relationship that makes us special. She was there for you. I wasn't. Does that make me cold and heartless? I think not. A lot of people didn't show so you would think 'fuck them.' Nope, not the case. It doesn't make me less of a man, you needed the people that were around. They stayed. I tended to the issues on my side, cause that's what friends do. They send their condolences in their own sort of way. I love my people, but don't get it twisted. I know where we all stand at the end of the day. I sleep at night. I don't hear the phone calls, I hear she loves me, we're crew, but what does that really mean? You don't put food on my table nor do I put food on yours. I never knew the woman but God rest her soul. I have gained a lot of respect for you. Why? You're a strong person, and that never went unnoticed, you are and forever will be highly respected by the three of us. I'm not asking for forgiveness, nor a phone call, I don't need that. Truth is, you have a struggle, I have a struggle; we take it day by day as it comes. I'm over here doing what I have to do, and so are you, so respect is due. Keep all the negativity to yourself, cause it's not needed over here. It's a new year, learn from what you lost, continue to gain, try to uplift your surroundings, and be a better person. She was young. We all lose someone, we never know what we have until it's gone, take a moment and reflect. (R.I.P) To last year, let's look forward to something beautiful and prosperous and blossom into something we created as one.

Respond if you will, but I had to get this off my chest, what you have with them is your issue but keep the resentment you have against me to yourself. They have a lot to say about me, cause I speak the gutter truth that is hard to swallow. I stand on both sides of the fence and the love we have for one another is different. We all have our own struggles, that's why we all share a unique connection.

Fuck all the subliminal shots, burn victims and all, whales, jungle monkeys, all the shit is for the playground so let's get off it. Everyone appears hard as they will, we can't appear weak. I call all the bluffs, I have too much reality running through my brain, I'm not fooled by any of the madness. None of if it is true. Too many lies, too much deceit, and failure; and most importantly we all have lost respect for one another. I'm not asking for unity or for us all to rekindle to old days. I don't have a point intended, but then again I think I do, but what is it to you?

My Life

You can't take the kid out of the hood and ask him to forget everything that he has ever been through. Stop writing, how ridiculous does that sound? I'm past my prime; I'm a revolutionary, a pastor, a hustler, and I loved what I did back then. You came back and it lit a flame within me, a feeling difficult to describe, I felt like I could walk on fire with no sandals on. I could burn my feet eventually, but I guess I would have to take that risk with a love so special. Too many things on my mind, too many thoughts, too many dreams that I can't use to create this reality. I seem to dream about it continuously. Could I take you away from the loved ones and bring back what I had? I'm not sure what you really want from my life, but I also don't know if you know what I'm capable of doing.

I love you. I don't know what other words could actually describe the way I feel about you. Don't be afraid because I'm the only person that could possibly love you as much as you can only fathom to imagine. Remove the broken wings so I can help you fly, soar above everything that you think is impossible and learn to live free. You seem content in the life you live, who am I to take you away from that? Are you ready to take my hand in your hand?

I see a lot of things, at times I feel like a visionary of some sort, because I can't stop envisioning what could possibly be. I saw a lot in my past, as well as in my present surroundings. I paint most of my ideas out on paper in search of something that the world thinks is impossible, whether it's love to a higher degree. Love has no limit, nor does it stop. I believe that one people can give their entirety without selling themselves short. Mind, body and soul are you salvation, which the other is in search of. When it's found, it's a blessing; as they envision heaven to be, but have never seen it, only felt the painted pictures from God's bible.

I'm remaining attached to my dreams, as if I was a young child. Envisioning love so young, I didn't feel it at the very moment it lived. At one with my words, I find it a struggle to find the peace of mind in my heart. Concentration is placed upon making a heartfelt piece to have you stop dead in your tracks, and cause you to come to an abrupt pause to have you think beyond my words. Truth be told I have to leave it up to my words and your heart and its possible destination. The message is in every word you have to decode it.

Peace of mind is a lifelong task that has yet to be found within. Love is a contradiction within itself, music is words to my soul, and family seems the most corrupted unit at times, based on experience. I wonder at times if I ever cross your mind, have you ever awoken one morning to the thought of me? Have you ever reached out to me physically or mentally? "Far from Home" is in your hands; it's considered a beautiful struggle in my eyes. Life is full of ups and downs but it's how you get back up that makes a difference. I struggle between consciousness and sleep, didn't make much sense to me, a lot was taking place at the time. The twisting and turning in the many possible directions dealt. There is much of the unknown, too much that I apparently know, so much I want to know at this point in life, but you still consume my every thought.

Peaches are sweet, but it's possible to be overjoyed with love that you do not know. The beauty of you had my heart walking to the beat of your flow. It was apparent in our eyes that this was not meant to be. I could envision myself filled with the abundance of happiness that has me so desperately walking away from you. It's so easy to admit that that you are beautiful inside and out, down to your very core, but yet not so easy to depict the many flaws you have that doesn't fit my description. It's so easy to be in love but not want to give my heart to you.

Subliminal

Parents who empowered me to express my inner thoughts and deep emotions no matter the case raised me. I learned with my actions that I couldn't please everyone in my surroundings. I have kept my lips sealed unlike a few people who continue to keep up the chitter-chatter where I reside. I blew off the steam like a kettle on Sunday morning. I still awake to rumors whether I try to ignore them or thicken my skin toward an altercation. A part of me beckons to address the few who step in my jurisdiction and want to play a so-called game, which I play to win.

This is my hustle; don't get it twisted—I'm a visionary of some sort to these so-called peasants. You're not the sun that arises on a hot summer day. I come from a cool environment where I flick bugs off my shirt, tell children to stay out of the streets, and when I see your children I give them a hug and tell them I love them. Deep down in my heart, your mother is a disgrace; your father is a pathetic excuse of something I see not evident in my eyes but appears a bright sight in some sort of direction. She taught you how to lie by lying herself right in front of your very eyes. Your father left the nest to explore another nest across the way while your mother mourned his loss as if death had passed her by. He was tending to another woman as he comforted her in her sanctuary. She decided to take matters into her own hands and lead him back into her arms, as she thought another child would allow him to appreciate the children he already had.

I promised to you two years ago I would leave it alone and I did but I heard my name arise from the most unlikely source. I'm only human and we all fall back on our words but this I didn't let slide at the drop of a hat. I'm excited to be honest. I felt like I could throw a few jabs at big foot and I couldn't care less what anyone thought. Childish? Not me, just confrontational to a degree, and I know what I can do. I'm back on my bullshit; punishing those who dare cross the graveyard where the demons await the souls of those that have perished or those who have no direction in life. You didn't come to visit the dead so what would your presence in a graveyard signify?

I was missing in action since "Far from Home" was released a year ago. I felt I had gotten everything released: mind, heart, body and soul. After one go around, I thought my life was done with and it was time to move on. I encountered a few issues, lost a few friends—some murdered, some fake beyond belief, and the rest just chose to walk a path of their own. No hard feelings that is how life turns its directions. The streets are buzzing on how I feel about the drastic turn around. I stepped out of the apartment a few years back, before that I took upon that role. I surrounded myself with your people, the ones who lied and said they would be there for you, and it turns out that wasn't the case. He stole your money, she accused you of it, and you taught your flesh and blood to lie to her own father, who she missed incredibly. An asshole beyond his prime, I would always be that person to pick up the slack and be a presence beyond anything that you could ever envision. It was just rolls that passed the time that you needed to heal those wounds that you suffered from day one in front of the bakery. They must have thought I forgot the importance of it all, every bit of detail, as if my heart wasn't there. He praised me that day for granting him permission to follow through on a journey he pleaded his heart to; I, in return, granted him permission. A few months later, a new life was on the horizon and I was prepared to go the distance and be that person as if I were that right-hand man. I dealt with the abuse of him not being around, friends? What do you have them for? If I wasn't the one then I don't know who or what I was at that particular time in my life. I ignored the non-believers, people who doubted you, unfaithful. I never left your side despite the rumors of you in a bathroom taking a litre in the wrong direction, bent over. What a disgrace. I stood by you nonetheless.

Back Then

Back then I told the true people who stood alongside me I would ride until the wheels fell off. A lot has changed since then. Different agendas, priorities change, situations alter, and people move on. These days it's hard to tell who really cares for me; too much switching going on. They say my heart's turned cold compared to back when I was that baby boy. I didn't ask for much but what I did do is make the best out of what was on that table. I helped build that same table, ask the brothers; I took in so much, as well as give. The girls from back in the day call me baby boy; I still think I am because I was not blessed with that life to begin with. As a kid, you believe once friends, it was forever. However our minds change, our situations affect who we are, the people around us change for the better, some take a turn to the worst.

My city, my side, my world, whatever you want to call it, I was there, witnessed so much that went down. Moments away from the gunfire, heard the gunshots when Fox died. Two of the longest shots that went down in the city in quite sometime, but I can still recall it to this very day. A lot has changed since then, back then.

I have to be honest at this point though I fail to neglect a lot of the thoughts that have transpired but then again this is always the case. I am not feeling half of you people; my heart doesn't beat to your flow. I'm painting vivid images and in the pictures I can't visualize you anymore more because it appears a distant image, my thoughts have become shady. I can't look beyond that image and spot some of you the least bit, it doesn't seem clear. I was told by a wise man to exploit the fake ones, and to some degree praise the real. I walk the streets uptown, downtown, away from enemy lines. Where the respect is granted, I still live. I hustled in Scarborough just like every jungle city kid did; selling the same thing every other kid yearned for at lunch time, sweets.

I saw beefs, wars, and the lingo changes everywhere you go but I adapt. I walk with the blade not in fear of someone taking my life but the fear of not knowing beyond that very box. I want to inspire and help transpire change but one day my heart will skip the same beat that awakes every morning. Afterlife is not a suggestion I attempt to solidify my status every day. He, who fears death is in denial, we live to die, bred to live.

I was told go back and find my heart, truth be told I always had it. When the grass is cut the snakes will show I got to thank my homie Zee for that though, I feel like he's been everything and more. Perfect time for me to go to the east and get a job with the madness that had surrounded me. He allowed breathing ground in some type of way not even he could imagine. It's not the bitterness; the hunger for more is what I crave. Whenever I carve this pen into this pad, found on the very doorstep I used to walk on. Daddy wasn't around to tell the stories; mommy was here and there, yet still I remain. I have turned my ears to the streets, eyes open to the blocks, and I have become blunt and honest. I feel like God opened my ears more to what young Zee said; I have become more subjective to his thoughts.

I was told that this is not me, if not than who am I? Who are you to tell me my dreams and aspirations? Tell me I'm hell bent? I don't need your love. At one point I did, but I learned to crawl before I could walk; there isn't anything that I can't do. This is not the way I write, the way I think, it's not respected to any degree. I'm not here to impress to the masses of people, I'm not a writer, or role model; look at me however you please. I embrace the criticism as well as the embarrassments that you have thought of me. Far from Home introduced new limits, it was out of the ordinary, it allowed whomever read the diary to see me for who I truly am, a free spirit ready to fly amongst anything that is thought to be impossible. I can't be recognized for my faults or opinions, I can't be mad when you fire at me, because what I can do is beyond your imagination. I can go the limits wherever and whenever, name the place. I deal the shots as soon as I receive them, no subliminal; I have my guards, think whatever you want to think. Pick up your head when you see me, man up, I got mine up, the respect is granted. I'll refrain from being like the young rapper who seems to think he's got a name, disrespecting all that is. I'll save him for another day. I grew up surrounded by the same people I continue to see to this very day. I'm not feeling your actions, your lyrics, I'm not done writing. I don't need the wars. I fight with my words.

From the cradle where I was rowed to sleep
Seems not a distant memory but yesterday
I grew through years of destruction and mass confusion
The truth never told very much never to unfold
So many untold stories
Distant memories
Displaced thoughts
Visions buried
Life at odds for god to lead
I know not half if not all
So much stress
Friends went their ways
Family members displaced
Life as a boy
I look back

I was introduced with no introduction
Revealed with no red carpet
Connected to an extension cord
The world seem so cold
Dark mysterious an strange
So many seem distant an fake to an extent
Many want the same
Same dreams
Same aspirations
Aspirations seem to be some belief
Are they mine?
Are they yours?
I seem delusional
I know not what I want at times
Your dreams have me jaded

Sky seems not the limit for me
There seems to be no end
It seems never ending
For some life is never ending
Always a remembrance
As the soldiers died for our freedom
They must be remembered
As does I
To that degree
To that comparison
I've done nothing to that extent
I've been myself
Never soliciting my heart
My pain is inevitable
Feel me

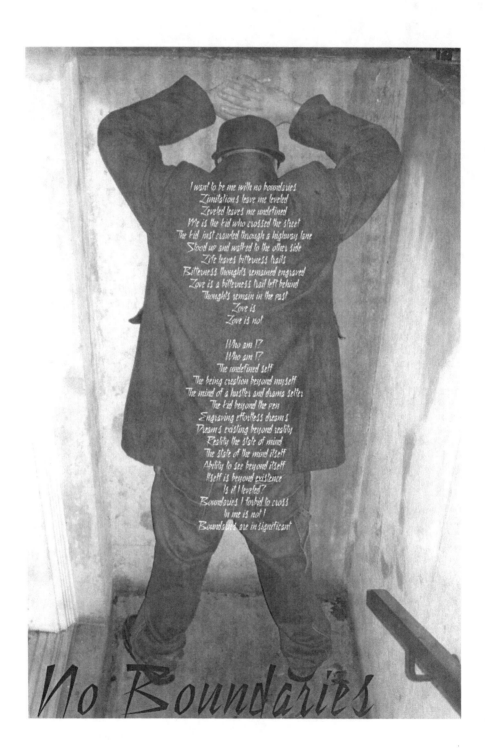

I want to be me with no boundaries
Limitations leave me leveled
Leveled leaves me undefined
Me is the kid who crossed the street
The kid just crawled through a highway lane
Stood up and walked to the other side
Life leaves bitterness trails
Bitterness thoughts remained engraved
Love is a bitterness trail left behind
Thoughts remain in the past
Love is
Love is not

Who am I?
Who am I?
The undefined self
The being creation beyond myself
The mind of a hustler and drama setter
The kid beyond the pen
Engraving effortless dreams
Dreams existing beyond reality
Reality the state of mind
The state of the mind itself
Ability to see beyond itself
Itself is beyond existence
Is it leveled?
Boundaries I forbid to cross
In me is not!
Boundaries are insignificant

No Boundaries

Everything seems not the same
But different
A lot has changed since then
The eagle seems to fly repeatedly
Death seems sure so young
I have not a clue
I know not inkling
Life seems so pitiful
Such a price to pay
So many souls been taken
At war with these odds
Courage is always to have
My grave seems near by
I know it is eminent
I await not that day
I am prepared

I remember the nights under the streetlights
The fights in the yard
Jumping the fence
I am no boy
Born to crawl I could walk
I could run
The sirens and the crew
Memories
The clock ticks
A baby is born
Containing a place in this world
Where it is dark
Hell though hot
Church is peaceful yet safe
The lord seems here at times
Others not
The lines appear not straight
He made it not the way
Your way
Its way
Not given
Two words
Your choice

I've been critically acclaimed
To publicly ashamed
Wished death upon
Given words of inspiration
Been an inspiration
They heard me speak
A lyricist a mentor
A brother a Negro
Played judgment upon
A dying breed
I will die on my bloody leave
Infiltrating the weak
Giving to those who seek
I have yet to reach my peek

Before we enjoy the sun
We must first live through the rain
Endure the pain
Agony and suffering
For this is reality
This is real talk
Real life

Life as it is
What it appears to be
An allusion
So deep and strange
No more sleep in my eye
I see the world clearly
I reminisce and remember
Hard times are a walk away
The realness is within
I'm tired
Whether it be the frustration or hunger
It keeps me going
It isn't the same no more
Changing everyday
My thoughts and vision
On a mission
I know not enough
If not all
What I know
I don't
Life as is
An illusion

Ink seems to be my pacifier
My source of oxygen
Can I vent?
Let me breath for a minute
My source of inspiration
Seems my conscience
My conception seems deep
I seem filled with optimism
As I write a composition
Easing my pain
Quenching some thirst
Suppressing my hunger
My conception
I have to let it go

I remain enthusiastic through pain
Though he remains shackled on the bus
Though he thinks he is suppressed
Though he fights over a cell
As if it were home
He remains a mystery of some sort
That donor appears nobody
I walked with no shoelace
I've walked barefoot
I sold chocolates
I slept on the porch
In the back of a car

I could never lose the love of the streets that endeared me
It has made me wise and able to see
I am a blue bird
A city boy
Clearly a superior breed
Amongst so many
A dying breed yet to be born
A generation a corrupted
This life seems trifling
Some starve
While others bleed to eat
I reminisce confinement
I seem confined
My world seems confined
I seem confined by my world
I remain enthusiastic through pain
My world seems clear
My world is jaded

Coming from where I'm from
Fatherless homes
Common as police who hate us
For the color of our skin
Oppressed they had them
Legal hustle
Illegal hustle
Life born a struggle
A belief in distant destiny
So eager to chase a dream
So eager to escape reality
R.I.P or hard sentenced
Facing adversity immeasurable odds
Living for that night
Awaking not at early morning
Robbing the brinks a goal
Nothing comes free
Hard work and perseverance
Coming from where I'm from
My home
My jewel

My heart goes out to the homeless and poor
The people up state incarcerated
Seeking life as we know
To everyone who was committed
It's ok to sweat tears
Life can be one fear
The worlds a song
It's just lost its verse
To the less fortunate
Seeking life beyond
Only knowing life before their very eyes

I can't protect you from pain
Nor shield you from the world
Nor stop the shots
Nor can I catch all the tears
It's a part of life
Death is inevitable
Life's as real as it gets
I control so little
Only can I do so much
I love you
Though that's not enough

Look in his eyes see no pain
Remember the days left astray
A bondless cub you thought
Cub out of wedlock
Left out in the street to roam
Walking the road of no direction
Not at loss your humility
Your passion a nut
Away from that nut something inconspicuous
Such a thing can hatch and blossom
As if it were a flower
Though it grew with time
Flower as it appears
A man so it seems
I am

You scream war
I scream peace
I promote peace
I love you
Life is you
Life I love
War you condone
Life, life, life
War, war, war
Three big words
It's very simple
I love you

I remember more than the seldom
I remember if not too much
Tsunami victims
To all the people who died in that plane crash
All the families that mourn there loss over 9/11
I saw the planes no witness
I was graced with images
I felt the tears as If was there
Though not a dream I was a part
This is not a gift
This is god given
I was blessed to write as is to live
So I shed my blood sweat and tears
If I may
If I might
Listen to these words on this night

The bombs keep dropping
The world is at a stand still
Lebanon is being destructed at will
There's war in the Middle East
Plains are coming from the south
I listen the news as they run their mouth
In the paper they cross the bridge
People in Canada got nowhere to live
Birth rate rises
So do the number of guns
When are we going to stop these people from coming from the
    slums?
I'm not oppressed nor is the world
There is opportunity for every man, woman, boy, and girl
I'm alive I shout to the many people
We have different eyes
But at times not equal
Been there, done that
A line from the past
People want me dead in my casket
Last words at last
I'm not dead yet
Nor heaven found
God has his plan
I stay steady wearing his crown
I'm a king, a prince
A vision in your eyes
Close your eyes to some
I am an angle in disguise
I walk the roads
Listening to silent rain
Dreaming and wishing of things that can never be
The street seems foggy

Not many lights to guide me
I'm weak at times
Though sometimes stiff
God we see me through along with his lift
People struggle to find a sense of passion
A sense of hope
Look deep within
With that big scope
Your heart will see you through the thickest of things
As long as you believe
What these clouds may bring
Accepting reality more and more each day
I remember the past when I use to shoot clay
No longer a man
I'm far from home
Help me find my steps
As continue to create this dome
Dome full of thoughts that I continue to express
I'm free at last but nonetheless
I keep writing to touch souls with my words
Maybe the first, maybe the second definitely the third
I'm kicking down doors at will
Breaking barriers with every leap
The puddles however seem steep
I'm drowning at times
Or so I think
I'm awake with just a blink
Is this a dream or reality itself?
I sit back up only to sink
In the many thoughts that appear to help
Gone am a gone?
Forgotten will I be forgotten?
It's up to you

As I say goodbye briefly
Only to touch your heart again
In some other way profound
For me not my soul parishes to the ground

Five foot 5 wit brown eyes
Body built like a woman over 25
Words from musiq soul child
A beautiful woman yes indeed
At a loss for words I suppose
What should I say?
What should I do?
Poetry is not the way
How can I be real at 22?
Relatively young
Such a stage to overcome
How can I be real?
To such flower
How do I address her beauty?
Shall I refrain from being deep?
Shall I not be kind?
What would she say?

What remains apparent

Seems transparent

I remain a vivid image

A rose that grew from concrete

An unknown leaf drifting in the wind

As the other leafs drift away with the wind not blowing in there
    direction

Defining my own direction

At not one with the wind

But my life itself

Redefining my own steps of action

As a baby I didn't crawl

As a baby I was born on my feet

Or so it seems as I look back

What seemed transparent

Is now apparent

France I only know by a dream
I know not the world
But my own world
I know not your world
I know my words
Words that whisper
Words that shout
Words that I myself embrace
To an extent I know your words
I know not your heart
I know your smile
That I have seen
My smile
At times I smile very little
From ear to ear
Or how is it performed again?
I once knew my touch
Or how do I touch?
Touch like never before?

Ashes to ashes
Dust to dust
I remain alive
In my own words I testify
I'm not in Vietnam
Nor am I in Sierra Leon
I have my arms as well my legs
Though I cannot feel their pain
I represent something to which I believe
I refuse to give my heart away
Accept in my words
I will not sink like that boat across sea
I will not die before my voice is heard
Parliament will hear me
The world will hear me
My words will never die
Can I live?

Five foot five light brown eyes
Body built like a woman over twenty five
Numbers are no comparison to a beauty this deep
I five means nothing just a number
So I grace u with my words
A smile means so much
As much as touch close as a feel
A warm heart I sense it
Though I cannot feel
A blush as she says
That I love taking her mind off the obvious
He has a good heart, his daughter within
Only faith can hold him so he survived
Let him live to see such a beautiful soul
A core built by beauty
From the heart of a princess into a heart of a King
Smile sweetness Smile
Reflection

Impossible to understand life itself
The many struggles and pain endured
Jus make sense
Look to the sky
Await better days
Watch the clouds move, as does life
Watch it rain
Watch the sun appear
Admire beauty
Admire a struggle
As it is what makes a person
Life
Beauty smiles an above
Holding an object within hand
Smile beauty smile

I recall because I have been there before
Boxing, shootouts and fists fights
From zone to zone
Bridge to bridge
City to city
Witnessed a mothers tears
A cry out for a fatherless child
I was one
I was his best friend
He lay awake at night
Not soul to tuck him in
He snitched I cried
He needed closure
Deep down a hunger for acceptance
A fatherless child his mother cried
Bridge to bridge
City to city at all odds
Still to succeed

A glance, the wink of an eye
A blessing in disguise
Can she be as she appears?
Heaven sent soft-spoken words in my ear
Should I rhyme?
Can I speak?
Could this be love?
Or does she just have me weak
So many thoughts
The aspirations the many dreams
Is she what floats down loves unknowns stream
So many questions so little to float by
Her deep beauty I cannot deny

Inspirational
More than words
Should I take a time out lets reflect
Beauty itself
A mountain so high
Her love is beauties peak
Her love seems genuine
I awake to make sense of emotion
She awakes to the very thought of another soul
I a smile, a nod
Appreciation
She reads on as she smiles
Smile, smile, and smile
Sugarplum

The flow of my mind
At times enraged
At times subtle yet deep,
So far, yet sweet
Far from home
I await recollections as they read
The dreams made
The attitude and mind state it took to get here
Shots fired
Fist fights
Yet I live
Jim Carroll
My name among his
Not even an inch
I await the days of comparison
Until then I'll dwell in the days of separation
My words
My mind
My heart
My soul yet deep
So subtle yet sweet

No government knows pain, agony, and suffocation

I look from the outside

The bombs and separation, the families, the blood sweats and tears

I know not the half of it

Yet not an inch tall

I awake to a fresh breathe of air

Speaking with the words from the man himself

Where did I go?

The corner store, which seems a lot less peaceful compared to the
trenches

Baghdad is in a bag, Third world countries

This ghetto mind state

I see beyond my own complexion

Beyond any complication imagined

I'm a man

A boy to a soldier in my own rights

Copyrighted yet infringed for the world to see

A man of my words no guns, no vest

Simply me

I can't appear weak

I have to explain the agony and defeat

Never defeated within, have I given up yet?

A writer? Not even close a poet to an extent?

A free spirit I am, on call nonetheless

I speak for the streets

Never close, so far ahead of my prime

The words spoken, I remain humble between the lines

Truth be told I am the truth

No complexes, yes competent, no complications, words flow so
    street, yet so deep

No particular style I remain free in my world

Can I do as I please?

The system says no I can't compete

I hear them loud and clear

I remain deep

The complexion in the mirror says street

Ghetto mind state

A man on my own

A man of my own

A man I know

A man I appear

A man you see within you

A man I am I

A free spirit I am
I stand not refurbished
More than a product of my environment
More than society you see from your very eyes
More in society
Larger than life
I am that free spirit
Off safety
Lock and reload
Can I be free?
Should I ask?
To many questions, so little detail
Iraq, Lebanon, South, the North
Out far in the West
I stand close to the trees
As the leaves blow, I appear at peace of mind
Can I be free?
If I am, what more is there to life?

Up in the valleys
Over the hills
Where the flowers grow
The tree's wave at true love
As she walks upon its very grass
Kneeling beneath
For it is her very beauty that sets them free
Her smile sets the sun on its journey for the day
Shining light on all that is prosperous
The leaves blow the branches sway
In her direction
Direction love, sweetness, a ray of sunshine
Her words don't speak
For it is her vibrant body language
That's speaks
I am a tree
I wave at true love

A glance
The wink of an eye
A blessing in disguise
Can she be real?
Heaven sent soft-spoken words in my ear
Should I rhyme?
Let me speak
Could this be real?
Or does she just have me weak
To many thoughts
The aspirations the many dreams
Is she what floats down loves unknowns stream
So many questions so little to float by
Her deep beauty I cannot deny
I dreamt her smile
I kissed her lips
Yet it was a dream
Just a dream
Is she real?

Twenty-two years old
22 years fresh
Young, black, and gifted
Are my people left in bondage?
I'm not political
Nor do I stand it the City Hall
I am this society
A product of my environment
The system the problem?
To many questions
So little to little to judge
Am I impartial?
Am I fair?
I stand at odds
Both sides of the fence
Not everything is black and white

Remain content
So I was told
Raised a child
Yet never a baby
I saw the cries of a mother
The court system and disbelief
He did it?
Fire the shots Jungle City
Fire the shots
Shots fired
Man down
Man down
Repetitive as it seemed
Fox is dead
Ten got seven years
Shot seven times
Guns before books
Books before guns
What seems the way these days?
Never the case
Can I solve what I know?
So many questions
So little replies
My words
My life
This is I

Dark blue at night
My heart rages in search of forever peace
Its very existence, does it exist?
In search of the questions with no answers
Supposed solutions
Walk of life
Long roads short days
Death is inevitable
What be the cause of a soul to rise?
Gods call so the bible dictates
My heart forever lurks without guidance
Higher power, what be the case
He knows my mind, body, and soul
My inner core rumbles to breath
I awake to brighter days
Defining salvation to mind

The words are coveted
My heart spews with joy
Pain and tears
Feel me or feel me not
I am who I am
Like it or love it

My perception from conceptions
Disbelief or non-belief
What to do or choice
Left or right
Two steps back
Fall down
Get back up
Story about life
Never-ending but thoughts of everlasting
Things come and go
One thing for sure
Two things are certain
Words are the heart

Far from home
Lost little boy
Neither direction nor guidance
Doors appear no key in
Frame of mind disfigured
Words never lacking
Heart in the distance
Focus forward tomorrow
Yesterday existed yesterday
Today down in the back road
Around the corner in the coffee shop
He sips, glances, nudges his side
Tomorrow up the street
Everything seems the same
Change?

Behind bars
Souls do not emerge
Lost between the depths of concrete hearts that lurk
Chains are the sign of war
War the reason they exist in there very own existence
Throw away the keys
The outside world appears different
Appearing free it seems
Nothing seems free anymore
The prisoners are we
Failing to think beyond today
Our words leave us displaced
Our people's thoughts float with no purpose
Existence serves no purpose
Free is thinking beyond our own hearts

No hallmark cards
Breathe of fresh air
A son a soldier
A nightmare dreams don't exist
The heart collapsed
The faucet was left on
Bike left in the middle of the road
Who to pick it up?
He left never to return
Never said goodbye
He flashed a smile
Thoughts of what could be
What a vision to see
A lost child
Boy wonder
Wondering dreams placated by darkness
He can see but in the eyes of an angel
Mother nature can feel your presence
As only she could
It could never be possible
Can I paint pictures?
Can I see you?
I'm trying imagining your dreams
It seems impossible
God bless the child
God bless your memory
Its tainted in your mother's heart
I'm just a stranger who gave his words
A child to a child
A man to a child
A future father
One

I know not what to feel
For I have never lost a son
I can hear a mother cry
Though I cannot sweep the tears
It I s a leaky faucet
That has been left on
Rejoice not for his life is gone
An angel amongst us
To watch his mother
Walk by her side everyday
I know u hear me
I feel u listen

Resurrect my words when I die
The meaning of it all
Purpose in every letter
Feel my hunger for more
I starve for the best of life
Never afraid to die
Death before dishonor
Beyond the money and the people
I must live for something
Not living for nothing
My heart pumps the beat to the flow of my blood
Can I flow?
Am I fate beyond my core?
The depth of me is unbearable
The realness is in stilled within
Godson
God sent
A gift from the heaven above
Ahead of myself beyond my time
A revolutionary beyond belief
June is amazing
The brightness in her heart she breaths
Everything that is possible
Beyond the clouds
Reach beyond a star
Out of site
I am out of site

Resurrect

Godson
God sent
A fallen angel lives amongst the sky
He flies ever so high
He leaves us with not how he went
But what he meant to us
A sign of some sort
Let us be grateful to have known such a boy
To when he first walked
His first smile
Let us not live in grief or pain
Easier said than done
Feel my words
Hear me speak

He left never to return
Never said goodbye
He flashed a smile
Thoughts of what could be
What a vision to see
A lost child
Boy wonder
Wondering dreams placated by darkness
He can see but in the eyes of an angel
Mother nature can feel your presence
As only she could
It could never be possible
Can I paint pictures?
Can I see you?
I'm trying to imagine your dreams
It seems impossible
God bless the child
God bless your memory
Its tainted in your mother's heart
I'm just a stranger who gave his words
A child to a child
A man to a child
A future father
One

He blew a kiss in the wind
The day he left
Footprints as he walked out the door
Mother not knowing the look in his eyes
The last time they would be open
His eyes shut
Casket seems destined to take him lifeless
Jordan still speaks but in memory
He appears dead
His spirit still lives

Harper didn't return from his trip
A boy is a boy
Jordan had a heart as does the world
What makes him diff.?
Color of his skin?
Destined to happen in the black community?
To many questions
So little answers
Its still Wednesday it appears
His mother's eyes still blazed
Sleep is a nightmare
Dreams were yesterday
A soldier is gone
I never heard a politician speak
I got more balls than everyone in City hall
Quote me on that
I could care less
Jordan Manners RIP

Reality of life is harsh
We die by us living
Oblivious to time given
Life progresses as does age by number
Future is bright as light
Quest for knowledge is the beginning
What you seek is deep with in
Your search starts where you want to be
Where you begin is the destination you seek
A moment or step away
Make sense of emotion
Through sense of conception
In return you will see progression
The men at 6 flags should serve as a lesson
This is life
Or
What you make of life

It's the passion the drive and dedication
It's the dedication that drives the passion so deep
The conception seems sweet
The pictures painted seem vivid
I capture images
Moments are unexplained
Speechless justifies nothing without a tongue
My mind I hope reverberates over the same music
The streets hunger for a voice
A reason seems to be the point of living
Can you find it?

Lost in the words
The gimmicks over saturated
The lost souls seem to be forgotten
The memories live on
The forgotten soldiers voices are still heard
Remembrance day never forgotten
My words proclaimed
I raise no flags
I raise my right hand
Not free of anything
Free to speak and free to write
Sense makes cents
Cents make dollars
It all makes sense
New day
I awake to anything possible

I watched a city disappear
New breed
Flesh and blood died behind the masks
Masks of different creeds
Animals started to show
Grass never got cut
Snakes showed their colors
Nature resolved many issues
Kings and queens became oppressed
Streets died
Loyalty died
Crews divided and conquered
Hands fell
Any means defeated purposes
A city disappeared
Long beyond my reach

No talent
God's gift
God sent
God living
Justice due
2 words
Simply amazing

Creating classics through metaphors
Sleep is non-existent
Dreams appear eyes open
Eyes shut as I walk
Many thoughts awake me to darkness
Veins bleed no silence
Words are not abrupt
Outspoken individual no more
Speak now or forever hold your peace
For I am not dead
My soul never to be weak
I shall speak
Feel me

Society has yet to see me
The words and many scriptures
I don't make dollars
I converse sense
Visuals I construct
Monuments I build
I write on walls
Ink pours through the pen
My thoughts are a leaky faucet
Refusing to continue dripping
Not just for the cause
Lyrically and spiritually
Breaking damns
Creating sense of emotion

Tear down the buildings
Rebuild the bridge
Tear down the red stops signs
Let there be light
Pave over the yellow lines
This is what they know
A testament to which they are
Beings in the core of there very heart
Graffiti and wall structures
Blue black and green
Red rum
Red rum

The streets remain oblivious to pain
People crumble to there very knees
Souls drenched
Hearts begin to weaken
Lives shattered

Systems built on beliefs
Religion held in high praise
Clap your hands and rejoice
Lift every voice
Bibles built on stories
Forgetting structures
How life began itself
Notion to Islam
Holy sanctions of Christ
Jesus
God's son
Who am I?
Built within a system
Failing to conform to society
A being in my own right
Blessed with words and a voice
Heart and soul
My own beliefs
Surviving in my own structure
My life
As you see

My love is real
Some earn it
Some unworthy
Some walk with such intentions
Such thoughts to hurt me
I walk with smile
Though I remain in denial
Consumed with the essence
Essence alluring the true me
Many blind to see the true me
Symphony remains to play
To the curtains close
I have yet to receive my last call
My life never to pause

I want to ease the minds
Contained in every line
Spread my wings
So I can fly
Scriptures so deep
My lines become engraved
Forever to be saved

World outside my window
Girl in the windowsill
She steers peacefully
My thoughts
Soft-spoken words
Steering vividly into her eyes
My mind at paradise
Calm, breeze, short waves
Such a love so distant
A mountain can move a man
A dozen roses a sweet card
Couldn't help u escape the scars
Upstairs your sweetheart
Up above steers inspiration, love, and desire
A love to blossom
An egg to hatch
I can't conceal every patch
A promise to this
This red rose will never die
My word you can conceal
My love everyday forth I shall reveal forever more

Can I grace the stage?
Amongst the elite
Feel my words
Hear me speak
I speak vibrant thoughts
Turn up your speakers
Stay in tune
I have yet a clue
No rhythm some rhymes
A man on a moon
His own sky
Amongst the clouds
Storms brew
Sunny skies always lurk
Words change as if feelings
Hearts forever moved
I be that voice

Trying to take the world by storm
As I sit under a rock
Told me I couldn't speak
Cut off my tongue
I talk with a lisp
I smile and rhyme funny
Some refrain from speaking
Lost a few soldiers
One shot, two shot, three shot
Back to the hood
Concretes and stop signs
Bullets rain wars
Bullets rain roars
I continue to be shunned amongst the presence
Poets, authors, and extremist
Detours as I attempt to find a route
Under the rock out onto the grass
Fresh greens
Fresh greens

I put it in ink
I remain strong more powerful than Malcolm
No disrespect
I hear the blasts
I live in this world of wars, disputes, and words
I remain at one with myself
I faulter at times with such a big heart
I become too deep
A solid figure on the outside
I cry on the inside
I miss love so much
I miss the past love
I create too much these days
To which I cannot bear
Its not always black and white these days
The world is more intertwined
The roots pierce deeper

I wish I could love you
Like I use to love her
I wish a lot to be not like me
Dead rather than alive
Much easier to be a spirit than such a soul
I lost a Lego piece
Though I love a Rego piece
Felt I lost half my heart
I'm losing too much
My heart moves to different beats
The sides seem situated
I remain alone to walk a lonely road
They think I have no heart
Truth be told to big
My heart stretches beyond the earth's surface
If I left why does it feel this way?
What happen to the love and passion I lost?
Too much questions but I wish you would fight for me
I think I'm asking for too much

I'm just tired of living
The poverty I want to end
I want to clear the sky
Clean the tunnels so my people can walk
Clean the streets so my people can live
Turn off the leaky faucet
I wish my words would touch souls
I wish I could be heard
I think I'm asking for too much

The streets love me
The people adore me
Outside my realm I can still live
Love, walk, talk and breath

Can I sell my words?
I just want to be heard along with the register
I'm only human so I do contradict
The ink never falls back
It remains intact
Thoughts to mine
Thoughts to mind
Can I live?
Feel me
Beyond it all

Trying to envision
Beyond all the incisions
The love and the infatuation
The abundance for that very inner feeling
The word itself
Beyond the roots
How it strengthens the very core to create
The end of it all
Heaven sent or God's gift
I remain at odds
Beyond it all
Trying to envision
Beyond all the incisions

The world is changing as I evolve
The world is dying as a kid chokes
The oppression is building
I remain alive in witness to brutality
Creating sense of emotion
Maintaining devotion to what matters
Love is still in the air
I love my people no matter the color
Everyone is a product of being
God's got his army and were all his recruits

I love you
I love you
What means more these days?
Friendships are dissolving
I still remain intact true to me
I love you
What means more?
I love her?
What means more to her?
Inspiration is hard to find without love
Love is hard to find without inspiration
So what is inspiration without faith?
What is faith without the lust for more?
What does my well being mean to you?
I lost love and regained its existence
I still love you
Yet it means nothing to you

Searching for metaphors to define
Searching for creativity to exist
Exists is a thought
Existence is you in my heart
A dream is where that is kept

Home is where the heart is
Home exists with love and salvation
Deliverance from evil never not
I remain in good spirit
I love you
I love you
What means more these days?

Young with a dream and scheme
Eager the rise above the clouds
Out of hells arms
God seems the almighty father
I want to escape the threshold that has me confined
The thoughts have me oppressed in the territory
I am beyond the thoughts and not oppressed
From the inside in it appears
The voice is quietly heard amongst the masses
Words are passed around
Not through the speakers or through the wire
Read the pad it contains the images
My intuition and inner vision benefits the prisons
Beyond the bars and beyond the dark souls that are confined
Look beyond and in your heart you may find guiding light
Worldly logic is not the same
It is what you make sense

Young with a Dream

Love is in the air
A breathe of fresh air
Life's sigh of relief
A princess is beckoning upon early morning
As the sun arises as does her beautiful eyes
Paradise is yet a dream
Love is yet reality
Reality is defining life
Blood pumps the vain
The heart beats
Loving is effortless
Love is losing your mind
Love is compassion heart felt
Love is never defining but forever building
Building statures
Love is stealing smiles n kisses
Love is a hug
Love is forever
Love calms the night
Love sleeps to the moon and is peacefulness
Love never lets go
Through the night till morning
Love is

Behind the prison walls I stand
I stand a prisoner
Behind the iron curtains
Failing to see my existence beyond a mirrored image
I fail to see mans creation
A man beyond words
God's child
No firearms
A system in disbelief
A better man
Better days arise in my own reality
The sun shapes the earths soil
As the pen engraves my thoughts
Failing to capture what it is I fail to leave behind
Thoughts of hopes and dreams
Oppression will never continue
I still remain one man
One voice
An ignorant soul
A beast in many eyes
Until my demise this is I

978-0-595-51979-8
0-595-51979-2

Printed in the United States
120775LV00007B/180/P

9 780595 519798